STORY OF N-PERSON OR
I WAS BORN IN UKRAINE

based on real events

WILLIAM INC

AuthorHouse™
1663 Liberty Drive
Bloomington, IN 47403
www.authorhouse.com
Phone: 1 (800) 839-8640

Because of the dynamic nature of the Internet, any web addresses or links contained in this book may have changed
since publication and may no longer be valid. The views expressed in this work are solely those of the author and do not
necessarily reflect the views of the publisher, and the publisher hereby disclaims any responsibility for them.

Any people depicted in stock imagery provided by Getty Images are models,
and such images are being used for illustrative purposes only.
Certain stock imagery © Getty Images.

This book is printed on acid-free paper.

ISBN: 978-1-5462-7003-4 (sc)
ISBN: 978-1-5462-7002-7 (e)

Library of Congress Control Number: 2018914042

Print information available on the last page.

Published by AuthorHouse 11/29/2019

authorHOUSE®

"Oh, what a miracle! There is God! Oh, what a miracle there is communism! Oh, what a miracle there is capitalism!" Modernism is no longer an achievement. Achievement is the effective management of the modern world, which is dictated to us by anyone who has something to say for themselves; we're to make a difference has a time limit.

Someone who thinks that everything is complicated is very wrong indeed. Life is quite simple and should not be filled with evil fighting good.

Let's all work together and figure it out, because if we all overnight owned all information and had public access and influence on events, we could trust people to manage our affairs, and it would be possible then to build sufficient work for all of us, as united people with equality and freedom.

The goal is to achieve immeasurable success and widely surpass all expectations our society places on us.

What is happening in the world today is a terrible nightmare, Lucifer gazes from the shadows of your room and from every corner of every room in the world and praying to God inadvertently still leads us to the same fate.

Take your time, and think this all through, offer yourself another option. This is how I decided to act:
- To think deeply
- Nothing makes sense.
- Politicians have the right answer to everything that happens; it is either good or evil, Yes or no.

"to be or not to be," that is the question - everything else is extra.

If we do not begin to recognize our wrongdoing, chaos is inevitable, only the constant practice of training the mind, body and soul make us better than we are, without missing a single moment of our lives, without making more mistakes and instead of making the correct choice between what is right and what is easy.

Everyone needs to find a moment to reset for a future without errors, by clearing the unnecessary with the help of yes or no.

Our meaningless existence over the last 3000 years has shown no effectiveness. All in good time – Through nature, only now do we have a unique opportunity.

Thus this is only my objective opinion, and one does not need to agree with me, everyone is entitled to their own opinion. However, they are often imposed and are a combination of factors and influences placed on people. It is quite foolish that until now, we have not known how to master even the simplest of things. Whereas at the same time one could retort as everyone has their own opinion, not understanding that it is only like a husk or skin of a potato which should be peeled and thrown away.

Anyhow, I will try to express better what I see, and afterward, you decide for yourself.

Soon I hope we will all wake up from this nightmare and in the name of life, it will all be over, safely and with a happy end.

You are a master of your happiness - I disagree. Maybe in part, but the reality is we are helpless to most of what happens in our life, we are always under the influence of various factors. After all, what is life? – There are currents and swells in the river of life that which one cannot control. When will we find salvation? And what does it even mean? This falls into different fields of awareness and without also trying to understand the meaning, what it is and what it means, instead let's go back to the simple yes or no.

You can find the truth in the form of what is right and evil where all humankind agrees and sticks to "The Natural Law" - the clear standard rules from our instinct - how to be decent human beings. But to me, it is not reasonable that everyone has to agree to it, as at the same time one has free will, an in reality to think like this is just a fantasy.

What I am saying is that there is a choice for one to make, the rest is reckless actions that, with a share of only possible visions, can form success. These days our world is so confused that any word can be twisted and construed; because of this, success can never be guaranteed.

Centuries later, to influence the course of events or even to the roots change our very existence is what our generation is destined to do and is on the verge of discovering a new world.

The past is in the past; everything has been leading up to this moment. The realization of this should already have helped you realize that it is true because everything is straightforward - we feel the truth and purity of the idea with our heart, or at the most, we can explain everything with simple logic and I believe there is nothing complicated in this at all because of we all shine, each in turn, like the stars in a dark blue cloth going into the sunset. We will become a light that becomes whole, finding its path in this universe, in this life and in our time.

Someone will tell a story, and we will understand the awareness of the reality like an adequately tuned system of being, along with the economy, politics, and society where everything in one's mind has a right action - independently defined by all, individually and self-sufficient already.

A specific series of answers will abound from the work of any action when a person remains completely free, is independent, honest, and right in his choice. In knowing this, you can be sure that it will follow the concept of being formulated for society, which because of these decisions ultimately leads to one becoming a self-sufficient, holistic organism that is capable of many great things.

Utopia in the life of all and to the benefit of us as a concept of life? – "Yes! God granting" - this is the answer everyone would say, at a universal referendum of people for our future and the future of our planet.

Of course, it is only after detailed planning of all issues that we will all see if we are creating the a system that we all deserve, where we forge our destiny and our happiness and at the same time are free within the framework to which we agree.

The framework is:

- Do not kill
- Do not steal
- Do strong work
- Utilize robots etc.

Modern technologies can be given to us for each person to reveal their potential indeed, their capabilities and, most importantly, to become who you want to be.

For example: Hold your relatives dear, so that they remain forever with you. Have children, and those who have children ensure they keep their parents close.

You never know what opportunities can lead to right actions.

How do I know? - The pain in our lives from the beginning to end does not let me forget about it. But there is another way. Therefore, as is said above, this may be inevitable due to scientific and technological progress. Maybe we all live and must die to be free from our body, from the suffering on earth that awaits us from childhood.

Of course, one cannot understand all the possibilities of heaven and hell that religion has prepared for us, or the forces that will take us away and which control the existence of all life on our planet and in the universe.

The path that society must build for itself must be such that the people of all the earth are equal and know that there are not those who are higher than themselves.

Japan is already ready to make robots and personal slaves for each of us, they can write articles, count, and, in general, do anything we like, with various settings inside. If we do not start to solve this issue, all that people are waiting for is until they can afford such machines that will be able to manage their business, then reach a new level of power in the world.

Until the number of people in this world becomes acceptable and sustainable and poverty eradicated, many more people will unfortunately and inevitably die.

There are many simple ways to change and adjust the birth rate, to ensure the life of people in general, disregarding currency or passports.

And the energy in its essence can already be free for everyone if you place solar batteries in Africa, as Hitler wanted to do for his purposes.

When we no longer see the difference in the exchange rate for currencies, this or that country, then it is possible for every person to develop to the degree of talent with which he or she possesses.

Because it is this person who would like to do in or not or not does anything, although the person himself will understand, he still wants to do something, but at least he will not be put down, everything which we are so dependent on now.

In this reality, I believe it may even help to get acquainted with God, to whom we must say - we did not unite.

Even after we started to speak different languages and set up society so that all lived by God's laws and served truthfully, honestly, in freedom and with kindness. Kindness, from which all manifestations are to conveyed to us.

Through religion, from the beginning of those times that we love, where our state was called Rus and the young country with its capital in Kiev, and its twin city and its fraternal people Novgorod, had a great goal and dream, but no matter how strong and tempered with war Rus became, she nor any another vast empire could withstand the onslaught of time.

There was a Khan who, having reached Kiev with his wild horde, was so surprised with what he saw that he took off his hat, and ordered that he only take a ransom and not destroy the city. Over time, from the true Rurik, only Danilo Galitsky remained.

On the eastern lands, evil was founded. And under these evil wild tribes and their power were no less savage than the fair-skinned peoples and part of the Slavs in Novgorod.

Since the Mongols did not have their magnificent history, they are known for how they cunningly set over big cities to rule and how the youth were expelled from Russia for a long time in those wild lands before becoming one of the descendants of the Rurik people.

Of course, they were all from this new tribe and were not associated with either Russia, Rurik, or Christianity. Evidence of this became clear after a while and thus the angry haughty Moskalik.

He decided to take revenge on the raid on Kiev for his ancestor so that even the head of our faith of Kiev- Constantinople had to flee, stealing an icon along the way that until our time is in the temple of those whose faith never subsided.

The city was broken.

Who would have known that this was the beginning of the formulation of a new state in the east and that the Kiev lands would suffer the same way again, another 300 years in the future.

A new country could not stay healthy without those whom they would consider their sovereign, whom the people elected.

Anyone, even after a thousand years of obedience, will rise. Therefore, there is no better or correct way than to go into the shadows of rule over conquered lands with different nationalities. The greatest the trick of the past.

It is clear to see how this country operated in the future, over hundreds of years, continuing its policy of war and keeping its people in poverty and updating themselves in various cunning ways.

For example, saying that the enemy has no power, except the people who are behind their borders, because only in this way it was possible to force the people to be united.

For the people to consider themselves united, they continued to steal the history of modern Ukraine.

To do this, they began by destroying history, then eradicating the language, because they could not destroy all of the Slavs of Rusich.

Over the next few centuries, people grew tired of how their land was being destroyed and how they were kept in slavery.

Since there would be no real Slav, the free-willed blood boils, and the pure spirit opens up in the bodythat the Cossacks created on their land.

One can't be a true Rousse and give the land to the enemy. Born in an area enslaved by everyone who is from the north, east or west, one who does not tolerate this evil become an unbreakable wall for his education, for his faith, talent from God, and ordinary people.

There were strict rules on the Sich, and not just what to start talking about, the Lyakhs and Muscovites, as always the story of your king is how the Cossacks walked. They were meant to come to Moscow, as a visit to frighten the tsar's Khan and Turks into driving out and defeat the whole empire of the Sultan with their skill, but the event came and went. We left the forces of the son of the Ukrainian people, the yellow water on the history of those who wanted us, somehow and the other take and enslave, when all of us should live in equality. The strength of the people of this drowned in the blood of the history of Europe in love, love for the Dnieper and the Carpathians, the Crimea and Odessa - the pearl of the sea, and the weight of the Chumatsky path (the Milky Way in Russian), and Zaporozhye is generally our salvation where the blood runs cold those who will be sharpening our teeth because we will break all those teeth, so that you do not even understand how and what is at stake.

This will not work for you anymore, because everyone understands the truth in their hearts. Here in the heart, here for all there is a place who wants to change everything and achieve the fact, where all people will be brothers on earth, for the time has come, Vika passed, and we have a unique chance to create land for people, and not for government, where people are not considered as people, merely cattle, which are poisoned by all things, and some people who do not even have water to drink.

During the Second World War - the most significant human tragedy, our land suffered so much. The war took place on our territory. Look at the Nuremberg process, and you will find out what the fascists did to us, find out about Baben Yar and how many Jews and Ukrainians were shot there. Communists, whom we did not anticipate, arranged for us two famines – the people were plunged into hunger, in 31 -33 years of high wheat yield. What can you know about our people?

When everyone wanted nothing from us, then we had every chance to fight, we fought for independence against everyone and equal rights with everyone.

We were hanged and tortured, crucified by Communists, for the fact that you had a traitor on you when you captured Kiev. They wanted to destroy us as a nation and create a Soviet one. We invented a story about brother nations under their rule - it's funny, although we know all brothers in truth, only on the whole planet. Valiant Red Army retreated farther into the rear, Ukrainian cities remained on the same level with the enemy, the city hero Kiev stood for much longer in defense than what was in Hitler's plans.

Fighting for the native Odessa and Sevastopol - they just threw the Soviet army there and lined the Palace with the unification of troops and alignment of the front line. It was further in propaganda such in the post of Soviet times that it is we who are to blame when everything was going wrong. I will not say who is who, but you have to answer for what was there with people than when you adjusted everything that you could have left us there, taking with you all our sons.

Bravery was not here, instead of forced sacrifices to overcome fascism - a regime that represented the conquest of all peoples and the rule over them by an Aryan race.

Our grandfathers won, so that we now have a chance in these generations, in the newest technologies, again and no longer with blood, and we were able to win freedom and a decent life all according to some rules for a person all over the planet.

Moreover, we cannot deny the fact that, as one USSR country, we did not even suspect of some non-equality between Soviet people anywhere in our country and this was our strength. The war between them is a terrible dream of those people and at the same time, our reality and wasted time for those who can look at us from the future. This is because, as we are already on the edge of the line after the crossing of which we will be in no part of all that for which we fought for them, great people. The Western World is growing ever closer in interrelations between itself and even with the countries of Asia, Africa, and the Middle East - blood is increasingly mixed. We are all without such an obvious kinship of the very different ways of mixing, and since we began to write down our family tree, there are brothers and sisters, whom only faith, hope, and love can deplete. Since we are all brothers and sisters, our desire can be healthy, pure, and full of friendship. The romance between countries for which we were divided in the struggle for power, playing on our difference in appearance, language, terrain, should not mean anything other than the acceptance of the fact that it was and is, but further either a real unity and a new life, or death and emptiness.

We are Earthmen- when the flash of light in the hearts of billions, each from and among all the oceans and up to the very cosmos, we are smoking all over the earth, how the fire smolders, and Occasionally, we were fired when everyone was unified to defeat fascism, but then, again, although the war is cold, we have not been united, we can go out back, and yet the fire, now on the Maidan. You know this is our last hearth, that there is a hope that it did not go out at all for of the whole world and is smoldering now on the front line in the war with the fraternal people.

Einstein created a light bulb for a simple life and at the same time for great achievements, so in the center of Kiev in the square all together this same light bulb uphill was raised to show everyone. We are here to create a new simple reality for all of us and also time to accomplish what is not possible, what has not happened before - to light a dream, so that the Lord will see us from the most remote universe and understand that there is still hope, to put light on the darkness. Respond to our ancestors, call off the hearts of the living, the power of love, the power of goodness, there on the front line in a hybrid war across the world - there our twenty-year-old nurse is dying on the real front, after four years of actual combat.

In Crimea, people are now under the rule of a criminal.

There is a war in the hearts and minds, and with everything material, there is a shadow on everything, cryptocurrency, dope.

Humanity is lost, and its time for us to wake up and find the path, to unravel all these webs, get a better life, and achieve what was not ever dreamed of before. Not only battles on the Ukrainian land, look

more broadly, but this is also the war on the whole earth, and this is about good and evil. There are faces, there is a line, there are rules, but there are hearts that do not have to think that these faces or features matter.

If you look at the whole history of our territory, you can see that there has been no peace, since the days of the Trypillian culture. If there is a mirror reflecting our world in all its ugliness, then this is Ukraine. All this time, the period of domination of evil in the land of Kievan Rus. It is necessary to stop and explain. But with this evil one wants to hope that in this world everything can change.

Why stop?

It is effortless. A little lesson in the history of the world that you do not know about a world that no one knows, about souls that are not understood, about lies in which people are swimming in is what the whole story is about, but first, let's talk at this.

Kievan Rus is the source of the beginning of the fraternal Slavic peoples, under the guidance of the ancient Varyag family, whom we asked to come to us and rule over us on the part of the the enemy whom we respected, so as not to fight among ourselves for power.

This was a small pragmatic step towards the goal for which we dedicated our entire existence. The dream that brightened already then in the hearts of everyone, but the chance has appeared, maybe even hope for an opportunity just now. Sometimes you only understand that this is your path - the victim of which cannot be avoided and you need to risk everything so that there is a hope for a chance. We are all egoists, and it's silly to deny, but the fact is that each of us is a unit in a multitude hour and numerical columns, and maybe lace embroideries in Mama's hands often thousand-year-olds.

People always united and believed that the time of honor, courage, will, and true love had come. When it comes to one or even two; it's a miracle for them, but also curses, because it's just a sign from above, but in that pure and beautiful moment of love, everyone is blind and so selfish because it should be available for everyone. Do not say that this is not possible - it is absurd, and there is no meaning to the essence of nothing! But we are all here and still exist, so the individual fact, that there is hope, is also there, it remains for us all to unite into one great love. So far this has not happened, people have tried to live, survive and, despite everything, let it be not for a while, but to transmit a a hotbed of pure love between the two, as a flicker of hope that someday we will be able to kindle a vast fire, Walt Whitman wrote about it.

Everyone likes to remember what happened and how it was beautiful, many even do not care that not everyone, because for them, it was a great time - a youth or a childhood. Has the war passed? Who wants to remember that something terrible? No one ever! Most of the life we want to try to enjoy, not to remember. Now it is an entirely different world, and everything is entirely different. - No matter about the times, there is an honor, there is the truth and should be from the enemy in our hearts to be who we should be.

Kiev, the modern capital of Ukraine and was then also the capital of Russia. Russia occupied at least 80% of the territory of modern Ukraine and Belarus, maybe as much as 15% of modern Russia. All the rest of modern Russia was a wild place to be driven into exile with Russi and showed a land that did not represent anyone for any interests.

The baptism of Russi took place in Kiev on the Dnieper River; people came there from all over the country. Now in the Pochtovaya Square archaeologists have found the whole old city under the square, but it is difficult to imagine when it turned out that not even the country and people belong to this place, that's what temporary came on the glorious Russian land. By the way about this Ukrainians, Belorussians, a small part of the Russians are Russians, and modern Russians in the more significant part are muscled. In Ukraine, for a long time, they were distinguished by their common name - Muscovites and Katsapas, that is, goats for stupid times even about themselves do not know anything and loudly laughed at them in Russia until they had to cry.

For the people to be free, they lived in an honest world and respect and the main thing in the world with other peoples and with the different world, for only the clearings, were preserved and revered among the other Slavs among the dead, and only in time all the other Slavs began to respect life after death and to whose God, even then they were divided into different parts - paganism, not understanding that from one God independence, according to the knowledge of the truth, and as far as possible in the sense of the power of heaven, in other things we are now on different religions.

Now only the whole world is divided, Although the strength of heaven only one. The Slavs for the effort to live in righteousness were rewarded with faith and the fate of the rites faith in God, and only as people do it, everyone snatched a piece.

The death of Mstislav in 1132 marked the end of the historical era, in which Kiev played the role of Mother's center of Russia. The period of political fragmentation, the disintegration of Kievan Rus into separate principalities and lands began, and led to a war between these principalities.

In the Eastern part of Russia, which in Russia was called Great Russia, which was the territory of one state, was more likely to be given to those princes who were in disfavor with the heads of the throne in Kiev, would have should that they were lands poorly. The people on newly conquered lands are not educated and without true religion. And after the death of Mstislav, everything changed, and the families who settled in those lands began to grow stronger and fight in the east between themselves. The armies that they had made up of the people of that territory were descendants of the country that was called the "big Tataria" where Finno-Ugric people. Maxit lived, Tatars from Belovodie - who are not at all connected in any way with the CrimeanTatars. As a result of impoverishment, the people who lived in the territory of great Russia, still vote the descendants of their Krechev, and I laugh. That the area of modern Ukraine, as Malorussians call, and that is suspended the fact that this is the territory was the center and center of Russia.

There live their direct heirs of those same Russians who are known in their baptized Rus in Kiev and great victories, long before these events when they unite in the east into one people. They could only hear of the glory of the princes of Rurikovich, who only ruled by those Reichs, while they, like a family who had sworn before the Russian people to keep a sacred vow, and not supposedly given the power of God on the government to set themselves whom they would not want to Rus.

After the conquests of Yaroslav (Khan Chingiskhan the second name, his son Alexander Nevsky-Khan Baty), the entire south-eastern territory of Rus - Moskalim.

The fact that the princes who were in the east of Rousse were not so connected with Kiev and did not see Christianity while proving the fact that the Vladimir-Suzdal prince, the predecessor of the Moscow princes, Andrei Bogolyubsky, treated Kiev in his way, having lost all the Slavic roots and being the governor of the golden horde. He attacked the city in 1169 and robbed him savagely, burned It, and destroyed it, that even the Batu Khan with his savage Tatar-Mongol army did not succeed in this. To all this Andrei Bogolyubsky also took with him from Vyshgorod an icon of the Mother of God, which became known as the Vladimir Church, is still the main church shrine of Moscow.

The Russian land, from the word Rus, from this and the people "Russian," but after a while, namely in the 17th century when over the last attacks of the free Russian people, which called themselves Cossacks that lived in Ukraine hung enslavement. The newly created Khan empire was built in the former east of Russia conquered the Slavs no matter how few of them there remained, and then everything great was formerly called the "Moscow Kingdom" that existed from the 16th to the 17th century until they renamed Tsarist Russia. It was at this time that the enslavement of Ukraine took place. Contemporaries of that kingdom now think that Ukraine is deciphered, as at the edge of Russia, and that they are not educated even in large political circles call Ukraine Little Russia. In fact, and historically confirm all the known practice of the prefix little, as the center of the source and mother of territories and people who live on this earth as the brothers of the elders and the homeland of their land, which is designated by this discretion. Prefix "Great," in those days were designated as rural lands that were under our authority. What is it all for, and yes-it's just words about the truth, which is so important, and perhaps it would no longer be relevant, so probably, but not when there is almost no hope, but reason suffering from eating disease and poverty?

All because in the 17th century Catherine II understood all the vast territory of her possessions and in her salvation and future hired a whole group of historians on the creation and ideas of which Muscovy and all at that time uneducated people began to consider themselves the ancestors of Russia.

The peoples started to think of themselves as Rusyns. Russia, as the name of the country, from the same and for approval was in this name and consonance and to confirm the inheritance was renamed in the early 18th century. After Russia since Kiev Prince Volodymyr in the 9th century has already opened schools, universities. Later Prince Yaroslav the Wise in Kiev and Novgorod, but if Novgorod was burned and almost all cut out the savage tribes of the east of Russia. Who was given a name to themselves in the history of the Muscovites by the Mongol yoke, then the last true heir of the Rurik people Danilo Galitsky saved and defended the Slavic people that fled from the Kansky.

Of course, it should be noted that in Peter, all the same, there is an awareness of what is happening. It's not for nothing that the capital was transferred to, some too many people influenced the decision of the authorities, it is easier to manage all the rest from Moscow because one city does not change anything, as well as one country, one person, one word, in their opinion.

To have future ones, one must know their past, but if there is no alien, then it must be created at the expense of others who have it great and glorious. Because, as Mongolians called Tatars only in savagery and customs, they were those of the cold east in their skullcap, and in the rest, both skin and mug was almost like Slavs. For those who wanted to be at the helm for more than one generation, no matter who would come to power, it was necessary to have all and without the noise of uprisings against the possession of them to make it so that the people do not crumble. The country is not mired in internecine strife, to become a shadow over those who are ruled for them by their same and their princes put by them, if there are not enough of them. Then there is another family for the crown or those. Who will come after them - the plan is ideal, everything is further in the details.

The details are the same as the experts about the skullcap that was handed to Ivan the Terrible and then on, and now it is preserved, and even Putin kisses it as a sign of respect, as proof of the strength that has always been and is at the helm of the Moskos.

Any obedient nations will always try to free themselves, how to make sure that the the newly-made kingdom is not later torn to pieces and everything next in the future to win if this an hour does not come out?

The option is only one; I can confess to my mistress, to make you forget those who remember their past and convince everyone that this is the recent common, and those who will resist killing.

And how do we know that all of them have not been forgotten or forgotten, because they have their dialect and completely different people, even though it is similar to ours? And how do we know that all of them were gone or forgotten because they have their dialect and are entirely different people, although it is similar to ours.

An adverb is to be eradicated, and those who resist to endure and hire for themselves and put the main over someone, and those who will withstand all the same, forgive humor as animals, on the hunt to surround, shoot and then only catch. But it will be rare if you explain that we are all one and go for us, it's like an elder brother, because we all won them gentlemen with our yoke, and the rest will read in history what we write, because you have power.

I like your humor and your ideas.

These others were at the time of the creation of the Russian state of Ukraine. This idea was so prophetic and ahead of its time that under this drive and Hitler began World War II attacks on Austria, Stalin was also hypocritical on Poland at the same time as Hitler on an agreement from the other side, like Putin in Ukraine with the same slogans. Volodya himself is still trying to persuade everyone in the common root of the Byelorussians, Ukrainians, and Russians in their collective past, as one people, continuing the theme of Catherine II. For example, he opened another monument to the Kiev Prince of All Russia in Moscow on November 4, 2016. Two years after the invasion of the troops and the occupation of the territory of Ukraine. By the way, there are no Slavic brothers and blood relatives there is not a common ancestor among the Slavs; we do not share science in this way - pure propaganda.

There are more than enough facts about lies. I do not know, let Moskali be proud of its separate history, although yes, there is nothing to be proud of, only Genghis Khan's stories, murders, war and the concealment of the truth about different things and the slavish exploitation of people. It all looks as if all have already abolished serfdom for a thousand years, but in Russia, they do not yet exist. We all now live in a completely different world, but believe me, we are not in a better position, here in America their people who are living in slavery. Before you the code of far from all laws, the purpose of which since the 18th century was the political line about the territory and people of Ukraine.

21-22 The Holodomor of Ukraine.

"It's strictly confidential not in this case that the copies should not be taken off." It is now and only now that people are eating people in the hungry areas and corpses are lying on the roads, we can and afterward have to confiscate church valuables with the most frenzied and ruthless energy, and not stopping before suppression, which it was not resistance, the more representatives of the reactionary clergy and the bourgeoisie will succeed in shooting you about this - the better. " V.U. Lenin

| 1627. The decree of the Tsar of Moscow Alexei Mikhailovich and his father Patriarch Filaret ordered the collection and burning of Ukrainian books.

| | 1689 It is forbidden for the Kiev Lavra to print books without patriarchal permission: "... you did not send us to the first one, you should not dare to type such books of new terms ...".

| | 1685 The abolition of the autonomous Ukrainian Church and the establishment of the Moscow patriarch's control not only over the church but also education and culture of Ukraine.

| | 1690 The Moscow Cathedral cursed and censored the works of Ukrainian writers of the 17th century. "The Kiev New Books" by Peter Mogila, K. Starovetsky, P. Golyatovsky, L. Baranovich, A. Radivilovsky and others, because the Kiev Books Latin delights claim to impose on them "Cursed and Anathema, and not especially purely Tregub, but also Muldhubo."

| | 1693 Prohibition of Patriarch Adrian to bring Ukrainian books to Moscow.

| | 1693 Letter from the Moscow Patriarch to the Kiev-Pechersk Lavra on the prohibition of the publication of any books in Ukrainian.

| | 1709 The decree on the obligation of censorship in the press of Ukrainian books in Moscow.

| | 1709 The order of Peter I on the categorical prohibition of printing books in the Ukrainian language.

| | 1709 Peter I forced to reduce the number of students of the Kiev-Mohyla Academy from 2000 to 161, and the best scientifically educational forces were withdrawn from Kiev to Moscow. Among them were Innocent Gisel, Ioanniky Galyatovsky, Lazar Baranovich, Dmitry Rostovsky (Tuptalo), Stefan Yavorsky, Feofan Prokopovich, Simeon Polotsky, and many others.

|| 1718 p. The burning of the archives and the library of the Kiev-Pechersky Monastery (materials collected over 700 years), which withstood the invasions of the Mongols, Poles, Tatars. The library was "... an extensive and oldest library, collected and enriched by the Grand Duke of Kiev, Yaroslav Vladimirovich, and kept in caves from all enemy attacks and ruins, but now ... among wealth and silence, a flame is devoured. It contained many thousands of manuscripts and all kinds of precious manuscripts written in different languages, and many of them were not known to scientists of that time, and especially all notes and documents on the history of the rule of the Slavic tribes and kings concerned the "History of the Russians."

Art. 303-304, form. 1956).

|| 1720 The decree of Peter I on the prohibition of printing in Little Russia any books, except for by the church.

|| 1721 Order on the censorship of Ukrainian books. Fines have been imposed on the Kiev and Chernigov printing works for books "not all from the Great Russian similar." Destruction of the Chernigov printing house.

|| 1729 Issued a decree, which obliged to rewrite all state orders and orders from the Ukrainian language to Russian.

||1731 Anna Ivanovna demanded the removal of the books of the old Ukrainian press, and "introduces science in her Russian language."

|| 1763 - Order of Catherine II on the prohibition of teaching in Ukrainian at the Kiev-Mohyla Academy.

|| 1766 - Strict order of the Kiev-Pechersk Lavra to print only those books that are published in the Moscow printing press tested and approved by the committee.

|| 1769 - Strict prohibition of the Kiev-Pechersk Lavra to print the letters in Ukrainian and the order to remove those letters that have already been distributed and used.

|| August 3, 1775, Tsarist manifesto "On the destruction of the Zaporozhye Sich and the attribution of this to the Little Russian province" and the closure of Ukrainian schools in the regimental Cossack chancery.

|| 1782 - The decision to establish a special commission for the introduction in all educational institutions of the Russian Empire a unified form of instruction and teaching of the Russian language.

|| 1783 - Opening in the Kiev Academy and Ukrainian colleges of education in Russian.

|| 1784 - Order to Metropolitan of Kiev and Galicia Samuilukaraty students and not allowing the teachers of the Kiev-Mohyla Academy to use the Ukrainian language.

|| 1785 - Order in all the Orthodox churches of the empire to run the services of God in Russian.

|| 1786 - The order to Metropolitan of Kiev to control the Lavra printing house, so that there would be no differences with the Moscow publications, and in the Kyiv-Mohyla Academy introduce the language, legalized for the whole empire, into the teaching system.

| 1817 g. - The closing of the Kiev-Mohyla Academy, the main center of Ukrainian culture.

|| 1831 - The abolition of the Magdeburg law by the tsarist government (judicial proceedings, elections of the government and local autonomy were subordinated to Moscow).

|| February 8, 1838, It was decided to open a committee of internal censorship in Kiev.

|| 1847 - Closing the Society of St. Cyril

Valuyevsky Circular - July 18, 1863

"Taking into account, on the one hand, the present alarming state of a society worried by political events, and on the other side bearing in mind that literacy training in local dialects has not yet received final legislative approval. The Minister of Internal Affairs has deemed it necessary, pending an agreement with the Minister of Education, the Chief Procurator of the Holy Synod and the Chief of Gendarmes concerning the printing of books in the Little Russian language, to make an order by the censorship department. So that only people can be allowed to print such works in this language, which belong to the field of graceful literature; Pass the same books in the Little Russian language as a spiritual content, both educational and generally designated for the initial reading of the people, to suspend. On the order of this was cast on the Highest Emperor of the view and his Majesty nobly was awarded this monarchy approval."

Ems decree of ALEXANDER, May 18, 1876, Ems

In the types of suppression of the dangerous, in the state relation, activities of Ukrainophiles, it would be appropriate to take the following measures accordingly, to the discretion:

a) FOR THE MINISTRY OF INTERNAL AFFAIRS

1. Do not allow any entry into the Empire, without special permission from the General Directorate of Press, of any books published abroad in the Little Russian dialect.

2. To forbid printing in the Empire, in the same dialect of any original works or translations.

3. To prohibit uniformly any scenic representations, texts to notes and public readings (as having at present the character of Ukrainophile demonstrations) on the same dialect.

4. To support the newspaper "Slovo," published in Galicia, in the direction hostile to Ukrainophile, appointing to it at least a small but constant subsidy

5. To forbid the newspaper "Kiev Telegraph."

b) ON THE MINISTRY OF PEOPLE'S EDUCATION

6. Strengthen supervision by the local educational authorities. So as not to allow in primary schools.

Teaching any subjects in the Little Russian dialect.

7. Clear libraries of all low and medium schools in the Little Russian provinces from books and books, prohibited by the second paragraph of this project.

8. Pay serious attention to the staff of teachers in the Kharkiv, Kiev and Odessa educational districts. They demanded from the trustees of these districts a personal list of teachers with a note of trustworthiness of each concerning the Ukrainophile tendencies and marked as unreliable or questionable to be transferred to the Great Russian gubernias, replacing the natives of these latter.

9. For the future, the choice of persons for teaching positions in the districts mentioned above will be assigned, about the trustworthiness of these persons. On the strict responsibility of representing them, so that the obligation referred to existed not only on paper but also in deeds.

10. To close for an indefinite period the Kiev Department of the Imperial Geographical Society (like in the 1860s this Politico-Economic Committee was closed in the environment of the Statistical Department).

c) BY A DEPARTMENT OF OWNERSHIP OF THEIR IMPERIAL QUALITY OF THE OFFICE

11. Immediately send Drahomanov and Chubinsky out of the edge as aggressors who are unfeasible and positively dangerous in the region. "[From the edge it was supplemented:" To be expelled from the border with the prohibition of entry to Yuzhny. Lips and the capital, under secret observation "].

| 1881 - Prohibition of the proclamation of church sermons in Ukrainian.

| 1888 - Decree of Alexander III on the prohibition of the use of the Ukrainian language in official institutions and the baptism of children by Ukrainian names.

| 1895 - A ban on the printing of Ukrainian books for children.

| 1907 - The government liquidated the Ukrainian periodical press, the Ukrainian literature was confiscated during the years of the revolution (1905-1907), repressions against the figures of Ukrainian culture began.

| 1910 - P. P. Stolypin's circular on the prohibition of the creation of "alien partnerships, including Ukrainian and Jewish, regardless of the aims pursued by them".

| "Favorable" on repression was 1914, the year of the beginning of the First World War: the prohibition of the tsarist celebration of the 100th anniversary of the birth of T. Shevchenko. Nicholas II's decree on the abolition of the Ukrainian press. Prohibition of the use of the Ukrainian language in the occupied Russian army of Galicia and Bukovina, printing of books and periodicals in Ukrainian; the defeat of Prosvita society; destruction of the library of the Scientific Society of them. T. Shevchenko; deportation of many thousands of conscious Ukrainians to Siberia.

| 1929-1930s - Arrest and try 45 figures of Ukrainian science, literature, culture, UAOC - for belonging to the Union of Liberation of Ukraine.

| 1934-1941 biennium - the destruction of architectural and cultural monuments in Ukraine, the arrest and execution of 80% of the national intelligentsia.

| 1938 - The decree "On the compulsory study of the language in the national republics of the USSR." and the strengthening of Russification of Ukraine by the particular division of the XIV

Congress of the CP (b) U.

| 1946 - Elimination of the Greek Catholic Church and subordination to its Russian Orthodox Church.

| 1947 - L. Kaganovich conducts a new "cleansing" among cultural personnel accused of "Ukrainian Bourgeois nationalism".

1951 – Publish articles in the newspaper Pravda against the "nationalistic biases in Ukrainian literature and art."

| 1961 - A new program of the CPSU proclaimed the policy of "unification of nations" and the further russification of the Union Republics.

| 1964 - deliberate arson of the State Public Library of the Academy of Sciences of the USSR.

| 1978 - the directive of the college of the Ministry of Education of the USSR on "Improving the study of the Russian language in secondary schools of the republic."

| 1983 - Resolution of the Central Committee of the CPSU on strengthening the study of the Russian language in schools and the payment of 16% of allowances for teachers of the Russian language and literature (Andropovsky Decree) and the directive of the College of the Ministry of Education of the

USSR "On Additional Measures to Improve the Study of the Russian Language in Secondary Schools," pedagogical educational institutions, preschool and out-of-school institutions of the republic."

| 1989 - the resolution of the plenum of the Central Committee of the CPSU on the only official national language (of course - Russian) in the USSR.

| 1990 - the decision of the Supreme Soviet of the USSR to grant the Russian language the status of an official language in the USSR.

-Can we be brothers? I don't know, but I hope so... one day maybe when all the people in this world be like one big family.

I cannot believe that I'm saying this, but I do not know the young way, and even through all the pain, tortures and rivers of tears that are not considered in dry facts, we must look for answers in forgiveness and in unity.

Therefore, I would like to rephrase the last line, not said: "I hope we all become brothers on earth."

We are all on earth people and brothers, and all of us are divided into races and countries of pure water propaganda and speculation or unfinished Karl Marx Decentralization in the field. By the way, do you know the peak of capitalist development in one word? Communism, only as long as the person in charge is not a warrior, is the only practical system will save us. Since even later in the 17ᵗʰ century, and then under communism, so this hour tried to do the s same thing – to seize Ukraine. ABOUT! Forgot to say in Ukraine the Moscow church does this, and they also think that their church from them to us, and not from the Byzantine, Constantinople branch where we should belong.

But, as Mom said to me, we should not judge or discuss anyone, and it is logical that if you believe in God, but when we live in peace among those who do not think or feel but have no choice for reasons in which, to be honest, it's not his fault. We need to all unite and take control of this world and create ideal socialism for all. I'm not afraid to say so, and the evidence is easy to provide about everything I say - this is no longer faith, God and his house are in the heart of each of us, next to honor and truth. God is not by business and the endless war. The first time we surrendered to Catherine Bogdan, the second commune conquered the war by themselves, but for a good reason, God loves the Trinity, this time we will rebel. The main thing I ask people does not lose faith.

Yes, we all went through this - were born and died at the turn of the century, at the corner of the next empire. All that was with us, that our peoples have passed and what has happened is happening again, not to describe and understand for you those dry lines a short historical note. We are dismissed as stupid sheep and goats, Russians with Ukrainians, Americans, and Russians, about Syria, and whoever is doing there. Like in Libya, Africa would be better off generally, but I do not want to be silent, and I will not, and I do not think anyone then he must remain silent. Enough already! This bursts out somewhere with a cry from his chest because you look where this God is and why he is so cruel to us?

This means they did not deserve it.

- Of course, they did not deserve; I hope the next generation will not be such a coward as all those who do not fight now, as they can, for the truth. To understand everything so severe, that it makes you sick when you are horrified to imagine how a Mother kills a child, she just gave birth and puts in a garbage dump. Here she is our land, and this is in the center of Europe, after all, that our peoples have passed, now everything is near you, only you all do not want to notice this all. Statistics, abandoned children in garbage cans, foundlings, murders are horrifying and so throughout the world, practically and this is happening now. Better your existence does not happen at all than to live so hopelessly, without sense. Yes, of course, to follow your life for yourself, or climb into anything in the world, so that God would like, it's all for the time being until it all touches you explicitly, and it will all come accurate and very soon. There is already a war, and your elderly, children, and grandchildren may not already have a chance.

I hope that we have already won by deciding to change everything, and now this war is inevitable, it is an idea that does not even matter who is speaking, just like all these billions of people that now live on earth. I'm afraid to imagine a queue to the hell of stupid donkeys that they do not understand anything and the same line that everyone understood but could not change anything, because of this world devours us all and feeds on our body and soul. Maybe this is the underworld.

I know one thing - either they or we. I think we will win because the world in this direction destroys the inglorious and the foolish of course, but the younger generation will notably support those who are still in the minority, and we will tear them all apart. If someone had warned me so much about everything, I think that it's better for anyone to start anything in life before they finish it. I do what I can, and I sacrificed my life for it, I hope it can help us all. I will go to the end for everything that has changed to save, and maybe then God will answer us, notice, help when we depreciate everything and gain, faith, hope, love.

Silence is not precisely the way out, what is mainly used in Russia; that's how you want it to be . That's correctly not the Slavs. But there is not only that, no matter how white, our USSR is so strange mixed up already then, and the next world, who to where. All the best minds in Novosibirsk for production, away from the war, the withdrawal of the Red Army to the very rear of the USSR, until we get together with the forces, as always in the human - it is necessary to endure. Have all our grandfathers of the world fought for this all? I think for what we could honestly talk and agree for everything about everything. I do not know how about this your Vova (PUTIN), but each person has a kind of space that he occupies. Putin does not stand out very much from the general mass of such rulers. If he wants to seem so right for us, to become someone who could do a great thing and then really be president for life. As president in China, and so you just Mr. President is worse than the larva in shit even not a human, as in principle and many presidents around the world. Either we change this system, which the system is not also easy to name, or all that was recognized and left aside and take up the real business, all together, all over the world, like good doctors without borders. It could have been dared, but there were so many tears and sorrow that there was not much that the heart could hardly knock on the pain and not any money, and power. Only memories at the turn of generations and a chance to change everything for the moment milliseconds that he saw. Mom's smile, Dad's eyes, a sister who hugs and hears her happy children's laughter when you do not yet know what kind of peace is really behind you at the window.

This is already watching the winter wind about how to sink your ship called life in this world, at least then that the soul then it is not even the wind. It's the night grinding and scraping its claws on the stern of the ship's horrific talons nasty rats that are trying to get to the heart of the living dead.

"Congratulations, you're thirteen!" Said my sister from the next room. Basketball, soccer balls, pears, and boxing gloves.

"Always be smart and obedient!" Dad said, hugging me tightly. He did not particularly like to show his feelings, he preferred instead to show his love by taking care of his family.

I was very rebellious as a boy, he was shaking my hand, and I jumped up and hugged him. It was my last birthday as a child.

"We love you very much, son!" They said lovingly.

"And I love you! Thank you, Daddy, thank you, Mommy, thanks, sister. My lovely Shea ."

"Here's a shout out and a song on the radio for you!" They added.

Oh, the new world! "Do not forget the sweets for the children at the school!" They added as it was a tradition to bring candies to class on your birthday.

My parents are diligent workers and pupils of the old school. Where honesty, teamwork, honor, respect and intelligence is the priority.

They were born in the USSR when people were proud and honored to be pioneers. These young people, called "Golden Age people," the generation that reached new heights, starting with the Olympic Games, the first human-crewed flight into space and base layer formed societies that adhere to the same principles of life. With an excellent curriculum and relationship with practical exercises to prepare trained specialists in their field - in which a man called his vocation.

For some reason, it always seemed to me that everyone was pleased then.

Our life is a change and a constant struggle in the awareness of our fate and vocation in this world. We are not only a generation, but we are also a country that can change everything - it seemed so in our childhood, to each of us, because everyone knew that we have a young country with a new young generation which was us. Of course, I was proud of my parents, and I was pretty much unhappy with how they might not take me seriously, because of all my mistakes. This is the problem of many parents.

Not realizing my achievements in soccer which I wanted to share with them when I happily ran up to Dad. He showed an incredibly low level of reciprocation as well as the upbringing in the development of children.

In schools and universities, along with financial education, how to handle money, etc. They should also teach the subject of parenting - how to handle a child.

Strange as it may seem, my first memories were very early on in my life where many people tell me that they do not remember so far back.

It was in kindergarten, where every morning I was the first to come, and the very last to leave. It was a beautiful sunny day at the end of Summer.

I played in the street with the other boys, and I wanted to use the bathroom. The street toilets were behind the garden house and these toilets were still an old model.

While I was in the toilet, someone, either as a joke or deliberately, threw a stone through the window. An ordinary yellow stone hit me right in the head. The next moment that I remember is how my head is bandaged, and a drop of the brilliant green with droplets of blood drips onto the floor in the first-aid post. I do not remember the pain.

Coming back to the cement path, which led to the playground where I got hit. I saw the traces of my blood the way I was running, and at the end of the track are my brown tights. Which to my shame, as a boy, which parents put on us while we were kids.

Now it's funny to remember how my mother screamed very loudly at the tutors who sat under a metal fungus with drooping heads listening to her. At that moment, I had only one thought that I probably was destined to stay alive, although I did not understand why. This question did not bother me anymore. A week later, the older brother of my friend in the kindergarten drowned in the river. I began to know that we are mortal, but I did not develop any fear of dying or any deviation in my development.

I loved chess and often played with my grandmother Dina after kindergarten.

In the second grade, I liked to sit by the window and to look at the winter view.

Everything seemed like an incredible fairy tale, more than that, in those moments, I loved Ukraine and her astonishing history in the struggle for independence, but since freedom was ours. For me, it meant that there was no more to struggle for, and that now we can all live happily. I liked this winter evening, writing poems about love for Mom, Dad, sister, Ukraine, and nature under the lights of the table lamp. Reading the Khobar of Taras Grigorovich Shevchenko, at the age where the book covers were still of his young face. I dreamed of writing a book also. Every family always had a book such as Kobzar. I even sat down to write, but I understood after writing five pages that I did not know enough about life, and that all this should be postponed, for some other time.

At the age of 14, I was already immensely grown up. Nowadays, any modern psychologist can explain everything in life, but this could not have been known when I was a child.

Because of all of my father's work, he sometimes would forget to pick me up from kindergarten, which for then, I was incredibly valuable.

I remember it was already dark, and I was left alone with a teacher who could not reach my parents.

My whole life despite everything, even in the summer I have never been with my dad fishing or hunting, although I knew from my uncle's stories that they loved it very much in childhood!

But Mom was too caring, which of course I hated, but I already went to school and came home myself.

While my parents were at work, I fought with my sister.

Sometimes I even very much ran around - not realizing that she is very, very much obliged to her upbringing and her courtship for me.

I even called her for a long time, just a nanny, and not by name. We were angry at each other, fought about everything, from shoes and to a machine with plastic pellets. The plastic pellets once cracked the glass doors in the living room, which of course, I had not one broken on purpose. I had to apologize and stand in a corner; sometimes, I stood up for my sister. I stood up for her because we were a team. My sister told me that I would be punished less than her because I was younger than her, but I believed her because I very much loved her.

We are taught to follow you and take care of you, but at the same time throw them out into the street. You will have to live separately when you grow up and think about yourself and your family that you will create. I didn't seem difficult. Forgiving me was hard.

I began to feel lonely in a world where I lived. Of course, we will never tell anyone about this, but we know that this is so - for some reason nobody explains this to us. We have to adopt such general rules of life and know that childhood will not last forever, that everyone has his way and with all of us sooner or later we will have to say goodbye and this kills most!

How can all this knowledge we can hurt our people and do not appreciate every moment? Besides, neither they nor anyone else to the very end prepares you for adulthood until the very end of schooling, but the fact that comes the moment is still much earlier, to take and leave to live separately, from the sort of like traitors, what they seem to us at that moment, it's also impossible and it it turns out that you are depending on them and sometimes even contrary to logic should obey.

I love my sister, and she taught me a lot and was a good friend to me. All I know is good in life is from her. She told me - I think, but what would Mom and Dad do? Probably in the family not without a freak, and with my upbringing they screwed up. Father - in the deficit of attention, which I began to feel free to talk about to people. They then did not already know who I was. When I wanted a motorcycle, he gave me a bicycle, albeit mountain and expensive.

My sister was already enrolled in the university since we lived outside the city. At that time, we became more closely related, and I missed her, even though she came every weekend. So Papa could monitor her, he was very strict towards her. And it only benefited me - I knew all the secrets of girls, how they behave, and why. My sister, probably without understanding it herself, helped me to understand why and how smart and educated girls to think. I knew how to behave to interest them, and they will like it. Already at the age of fourteen, when my best friends and I first went to a volunteer camp, I took full advantage of my knowledge. She was four years older than me.

Her beautiful name was Love. Of course, this undoubtedly my status with my friends. In the future, after ten years, I dreamed that I would have only one woman in my life since the quantity or whoever is just a delusion that means nothing and the main thing about this is not saying anything, does not warn.

Girls, as they do not understand. You need to know one thing, how you allow yourself to be treated so that you will be respected in the future, as a person or not recognized. All children need to know that whoever is poorer who is more precious is not essential since the main thing is who you and that you need to work on yourself. This is because then in the future when you grow up, then it will be who you are and who you know in education and as a person about life, but your family or parents are rich or poor. You still need to earn your own and be sure that your parents will give you the very best to start a life's journey. They are afraid of change, and independence is not worth it -

It's all, and all will come out, if you live independently of everyone, even your parents, in your way, but most importantly, as a separate person, then even your parents will respect you.

The main thing is to live in the present and appreciate this present and remember that every minute in life is a test and a test of what choice you make. Your task is not someone you like, even better if it's the other way around. As for children, so for teenage girls and small girls, there are no books about life, so much, everything needs to be done. Especially in the matter of educating girls, of who they are, the observance of their rules that they will carry through the whole life will formulate the next generation of male society. Every girl is a part of one universal education, which must be the only one.

I have already come to such a life in the course of circumstances, which I understood at that time. I was waiting for new chances to show myself what it was not, looking to the future I was waiting for freedom. To the best of my ability, I still played for a long time, but I knew that this was just a hobby.

It was great for me not to want to become a footballer anymore.

As if not a probable dream and at the same time genuine, I thought it could be football. I had goals about how I glittered in the green fields of the European arenas stadium. I was inspired by the Dynamo Kiev game, where they won the Champions League in 1997 under the leadership of our great coach Valery Vasilyevich Lobanovsky.

I remember when my classmate bought a ticket to the Dynamo match: Barcelona, which he drove with his father in the evening. Dynamo won 4: 1 in that match. At that time, I was happy for someone at such moments, and in general, children often laugh and live happily.

Then I started to go and play only in the attack as Andrey Shevchenko because I always managed to score well and prove to be in the right revenge. Probably because I knew how the goalkeeper thinks. Oleksandr Shovkovsky goalkeeper Dynamo Kiev, his phenomenal game especially in the penalty shootout series, bewitching and delighted. I wanted to grow up and become a substitute for him in Dynamo. My friends and I played with all the people we could, preparing for the most important game, between schools - it was class five. We were solid. Before that, we were able to defeat everyone.

In particular, my phenomenal match at the gate. And when the moment of the game came, without listening to a word of me with me on Sundays, the parents went to work without realizing that they were breaking my heart since I couldn't play in the game. I knew that morning that I would not forget and that I was a traitor because my team lost at a more extensive field 1-0. In addition to the fact that my friends harassed me. My dream died forever. When we arrived home, I wept bitterly and ripped all the posters on the walls. Then I realized that it was no longer possible for me to become great, although I continued to play for a long time, to score with anger against others. Support from parents and questions about the future of the child do not need to be asked. Though it's necessary to look at what the child wants and what he likes. If he falls in love, something that means he likes it.

We feel our calling, and if we wish to, we always the right to change its fate.

We considered ourselves adults at fourteen to fifteen years old when we drunk and partied until the morning.

We did not worry about our future. We became legends of our time in our schools and academies. At night sometimes I did not sleep, asking myself a question like "Why do I live? Is there something more important than a person? Did God create us? Does he see and hear me now? How can I check this? How to find out?

And if I did not want to sit on the Saturdays sermons in the church in the church where my mother took me, does it mean that I do not love God? Most often, I went with her just so that my father did not force me to do something at home! But when I moved to study at the Lyceum, I did not appear there anymore - since I studied now on Saturdays. Meanwhile, despite the questions asked, I often prayed, though still in my childhood, took sin at heart, daring to steal small money from my father, at first. He did not notice for a long time; then, of course, he found out everything I was, of course, punished. Though that did not stop me doing again and again, and once only my mother was able to keep my father from beating me up properly. And only one force is capable of stopping the child - it's not shame, not a shame, because he does not yet know this as a child. It's his father's gaze, which shows disappointment in his son, and this can keep from something terrible and shameful forever.

"Theft was for a long time in the past and not with me," I told myself, and since I did not do this anymore. I acted as if nothing of the kind had ever happened, so I discovered new doors to my life senior classes, from which he could take everything he could, probably. Competitions in all their forms submitted to us, we became champions of our district: basketball, football, volleyball - all this gave us confidence, strength, solidarity in training. My friends and I spent a lot of time playing basketball . We were the best team and already two years in a row.

We took first place in the district; I still remember how sometimes during the game I looked around the platform: My parents take pictures on video or look at how I play and where I'm the best. When I was nine; I was not allowed to play football against another school at the level of official competitions. Since I was a goalkeeper and was in my best form, I was even put on games against older guys.

My team lost one zero in that match without me; after that, I did not go to the gate anymore. I started playing only in attack and knowing all the tricks of goalkeepers. It was easier to score to others. You can regret that you do not understand. When one game is everything for you all in life and very much decides as well as the respect of other people. You can disrupt the poster with your favorite player - the goalkeeper of Kiev Dynamo and Ukrainian fencing, as well as just the right person and patriot Alexander. I so wanted to try myself in a professional football school from my favorite Dynamo club, but the lost opportunities do not return. The world lives without us with their lives, and We are not always able to decide our destiny, and even tears don't help - dreams of childhood wouldn't come true. Sometimes you can go with a principal without realizing that at that moment someone else's fate can be decided.

Since I realized that this is always the case, I promised that it would not prevent me from still choosing the direction of what my heart wants, when I will become grow up as an independent adult.

It was an unforgettable summer for our company; we thought it was the best time of our life. We set on the beach by the fire, went crazy, having fun, and to us, it was not important anything, except ourselves and that what's going to happen tomorrow.

I continued to pray, and He often helped me, and even finally, I answered.

At such moments I recall those beautiful times in which I hated music and suffered from notes over the piano trying to learn the next song to an academic concert, which still does not come to parents. I finally sat down and played for my pleasure. I knew that now after four years of torment I will no longer play the piano.

Of course, at home, everything was different. I often began to defend my opinion with reproaches and did many things contrary to instructions. Thus seeking and fighting for my point of view, which could be both wrong and not justified, but it was mine. I thus won my way independence, which I was eager to find finally.

Although my father and I were fans of boxing, which we watched once every three to four months, the Klitschko fights, which I was waiting with impatience to spend time together and rejoice in the victory together. Such moments were the best, and at one time, we were still playing paintball, which was in our garage. The best and best memories and whatever it was, I love my father, I respect him and immensely grateful to him for everything like my mother. Our family is our main thing that would be all understood this.

Sport made me single-minded, I went to additional math classes and as a result. I came to a high level with the right amount of knowledge before the last school year at the Lyceum.

I already began to understand much more than before, everything was great - our beautiful little town was covered with snow, which continued to go outside the window. It was getting dark early, and it seemed that day by day flies by unnoticed! Since our town was a population of only 12,000, many knew each other, and the political life of the whole country was not an integral part of all the townspeople of a small town. What is there to say also if children were interested in politics and knew all and all. This town was unique in its sense. I'm sure that there is no such anywhere else on earth, with its traditions and celebrations, it made it so for me from the very childhood. It seemed that here besides the life boils, it is together with that and stands for revenge and my life soars just here in the air. The cold air of the night sky with stars and very bright moon, with the sounds of the creaking snow under your feet in the deep silence of the town and only by the solitary sounds that visit the sleeping night. The day here starts surprisingly at the same time, regardless of the time of the year and the weather.

Everyone brings my friends and me, including our parents to the center to the Lyceum with an error of 3 minutes' maximum. We drove on one road since my friends lived in one area, most also in the same street. This time was so beautiful that I did not want it to end.

But everyone in life has moments that influence or change your worldview. As always, what is happening now is more important than ever (before or in the future). Often when the moment is past, we tend to forget it. But sometimes there is one more, a new moment that will never be forgotten - it changes your entire life and turns it around in every sense.

I was 17 years old. We, as usual, sat in the classroom, preparing for the lesson, when the Director came to us, or rather the female Director. Today I want to introduce to you a new teacher who will lead a course in psychology, get acquainted. This is Lucy. Me and the guys, as always, exchanged glances. We decided that this is a new toy for our games, because of which, teachers often refused to continue lessons. She was just as young as the others, fresh from the university. Usually, she couldn't stand our jokes, so ran out of the class in tears. But she always returned in a good spirit, for which we respected her and even fell in love in some sense.

And, of course, a teacher in foreign literature... "- For this month I can't name any of you who know the material with dignity, except for some girls, of course. The noise and disrespect that you show to me and my subject speak only of your bad manners. I do not intend to endure it so that we will have different lessons now, you will read the entire class and study the material yourself, and in the next class, write a test on the material you have learned, and so on until you learn to respect your teachers. That's all. I have no desire to tell you anything; start to read!"

But after twenty minutes, among the class, full of silence, "A5" sounded from the back desks. And of course, she knew what that meant, and it incredibly enraged her. She took off her glasses and threw them between the rows. She then gently stood up, took the bag, the newspaper she was reading and left the classroom. It turned out that she disappeared forever. It couldn't stop us from smiling.

Well, you guys! But I do not need such rules, I promise you fun lessons, and you can call me Lucy.

And she began to talk about the priorities of youth and what goals to have in life. She managed to not only interest everyone. But also force them to participate in discussions on the topic of sex and relationships in principle.

I could not even say anything and did not look away, watching her. She had hazel eyes with green and blue along with beautiful blonde hair. Her bright clothes brought so much light and laughter to everybody who knew her. It seemed to me that all that I had experienced up to this moment was not real. I suddenly opened my eyes to the world. The ice around my heart melted. My heart beat, so fast, like never before, from her one glance that met mine.

-: Well, the last question for today. Who considers himself a monogamous person?" She asked.

"I," said I. I raised my hand!

"Come on, Willy! You are monogamous?! You and I have known each other since childhood!" said David, who was sitting behind me, joked with me. My other good friends laughed with him, which I didn't even notice. I just said what I thought: "It happens, people change! But sometimes you know it.

In a manner not typical to any of my acquaintances, she said, "Wow, William."

"You know, today it's rare to meet a person who thinks so and even less one who admits it. Well, I hope you enjoyed the class. See you soon!"

Almost two months passed, we often talked with Lucy, both in the Lyceum and after then. By phone, negotiating various psychological tests, which were mostly carried out on me first. Then I explained what they are talking about to me. I tried to answer very honestly; I was curious to know what I am because I knew I'm leaving very little about myself and find out how it looks from the side. When I'm the one who I am and say that, that I think, without hiding my feelings, became my desire. We participated in various public programs, speaking from volunteer organizations. We together created scripts and having fun on the tests with my friends, but I knew them long enough to anticipate how they would respond and checked whether it was on the real business. And anyway, these tests have not opened anything new to us, and I did not need this, much more I was interested in my new page in life.

"Sonny, we decided to go for a month to the Carpathians. Do some skiing, drink some water, get well, grandmother and grandfather also go with us. Do you want to go?"

"No, I always celebrate the New Year with my friends. After you left me with the son of my son of half- Grandmother in fifth grade and decided to celebrate separately. So I'll stay at home."

"Well, Sash. We already apologized a thousand times; you're already an adult, so we hope everything will be alright."

"Is this a question?"

"Well, if you are not going to bring your friends and do not arrange booze, then everything will be fine. Is that the question?"

"Dad, what kind of expression is that? We, like all ordinary people, can celebrate very decently."

"I know how you celebrate - like last year, half of the cellar floor with the wine evaporates somewhere!"

"Matthew, let it be, better to drink good wine from Europe than this unclear urban drinks.

When my father left, my mother asked:

"And Shea will come?"

"She also goes to the western part of the country with her friends."

"With Bob?"

"Yes, but do not tell dad, "She asked.

"No problem. And do not be angry with your father, you know how he is with us, try to make concessions."

"If he makes concessions, then I'm ready for it. Okay, Mom, I need to study, call if you need help writing a list of what you need to take with you."

This meant, of course, that the guests would be in our house very often, or instead, they would not even leave here.

"Hello, hello!"

"I just wanted to dial you, then you called me."

"Yes, I also have this often. What are your plans for the New Year?"

"Oh, I'm going to Dnepropetrovsk. On the train! I do not like it, usually always there is someone starts to bother me; there are still some stories. I need to take pictures. I have a good friend to meet me there; he will make images fresh".

"Just a friend?"

"Yes, just a friend. Why did you ask that?"

"I just prayed. I do not know,".

"My parents are leaving for their birthday today. You should come for tea; you always wanted to visit".

"Okay, meet me in the center. Otherwise, I'll get lost, you know. I'm not afraid of the dark. I'm not scared to walk alone, but..."

"I know, I know. Of course, I'll meet you".

In the street, there was a minus temperature. It was snowing. This winter was unusually beautiful.

"Thank you for the tour of your lovely house."

"Thank you, but I would not show children's photos except for my favorite, where I am with my sister. You know, when I was a child, I loved drawing and writing poetry. Here, between the pages I just found one of the drawings, this is probably the only one that remained".

"Let me have a look. A beautiful picture,".

"I once wrote a whole little book, handmade, but one day it disappeared. No one knows where which is very strange".

"Well, that means it was not the time. Even more so, you're an economist. Mathematics is your field".

"Yes, but this choice was made not by me. Although I love the economy, but not mathematics".

"By the way, one girl would like to celebrate the New Year with you. What do you say?"

"I need to ask the guys what they think because we always celebrate with our company."

"What if I say that she likes you?"

"Well, it's kind of course, but if we think logically. This girl is from the Lyceum, which means she is younger than me. I'm afraid I will not have anything to talk about with her. I don't think that I'm brilliant. But she's just out of my league, although maybe I'm very wrong."

"Yes, you overgrew your age."

"I'm very sorry that we can't celebrate the New Year together, so here is a small gift. This is a Christmas Angel. He reminds me of you, so bright, beautiful, and friendly".

"You're making me blush, and do not look at me like that. I do not know how to explain it, but you have a unique look. Full of depth and feelings that overwhelm you. And, of course, I owe you a gift too".

"I would refuse, but I think reciprocity it is good. Alright, now I need help with my favorite thing to do. I need to decorate a Christmas tree on the second floor. It's a big honor, to be honest, this is something special that I always did myself".

"With great pleasure!"

"Look, you take a toy. Incidentally, this one in your hands is my favorite. You have to look for the place for her. First, by looking at the whole tree from far away and then without taking an eye out, go straight to it and hang it there. I'm sure you'll do well. I can be old-fashioned, and probably people have said to you it many times, but you have a lovely smile".

"You know, today you can rarely meet people who mean so and are not afraid to say what they think. Who are always extremely honest".

"Thank you very much, but I'm your psychology teacher. You should not talk to me like that".

"But we are not in the Lyceum, and very soon I will finish it. You will no longer be my teacher. I can't want to leave and study at university. Although I still love my home and my family here, very much. You know, I remembered a moment when I saw you first. It was about two or three years ago. It must have been you; you had a very short haircut. Your hair was some dark color. It was in the administration in the volunteer office".

- "Yes, but it seems, it was so long ago. I was in the second year of university and participated in one project. I helped children from orphanages, who fled and hid in the cellars of the buildings of the city. They sniffed glue and did all sorts of abominations. I spent almost two weeks there, trying to help them change their thinking. At one point I just got up and everyone who came out with me. They went back to the orphanage. I started to study to become someone".

"You're perfect. I do not know if I could do that; do something like that. You have a very kind the heart is beneficial".

"It all depends on the person. You can always change yourself, but not everyone can change. I have done many things wrong in my life, but now I want to be a different person.

I always wanted to help people, so I went into psychology".

"In my opinion, the Christmas tree has turned out quite beautiful."

"Yes, very beautiful. By the way, Max found out that I'm visiting you. he also invited me to his place, and as always, I and we lost track of time".

"Well, let me take you there. We all live on the same street."

"No, I will not go to see him today, better if you will take me home," She said, took my hand and looked into my eyes.

"Of course! We will go through a different path; there is a beautiful place. I want to show it to you!"

Time of this year was running out. I knew that in the new year, a lot awaits me. But now I do not know what to do because I feel something for her. But I'm afraid to confess that. If I admit, what if I can ruin everything, everything that already exists. And is it necessary? Does she need it? What's all this for? My parents were not at home already for two days. Suddenly the phone rang, and then again, but I did not answer it. Although I knew it was her. And so I sat through the night, talking to myself. Trying to cope with the doubts that were tormenting me.

Next morning, I was sitting at school behind my desk. I was sleepy.

"Willie, are you sick? You don't look very well".

- Don't worry, David, I'm okay. I'll be back good as new for the New Year's Eve. I'm just a little tired".

"What happened?" I heard Lucy's voice behind me.

"it's all ok."

'I don't think so. Let's meet after the lesson. We'll talk, I'm swamped now".

"Agreed."

But after classes, I did not look for any meetings. I just went home, full of confidence that I was doing everything right. She did not need it all.

I was already going to call the guys to come over when someone yelled at the door. Lucy stood in the doorway.

"William, are you all right?"

"Yes, I'm okay, what's wrong? Did you come to ask me that? You could call."

"Yes, and just like yesterday, didn't get through? More so, I was with Rob. I needed the Internet, but mine did not work for some reason and decided to go and see you".

"Well, let's go to the kitchen and have tea."

These days we spent together, always talking, getting to know each other better and better.

Sometimes staying up until the morning, not noticing how time flies. Only by looking at the clock, we realized that she needed to come back. I walked her home and then wrote her messages on the way back. I did not care about the severe frost. Something inside was warming me.

This evening my friends came to me, and we spend quite a long time, laughing and talking. I did my best to prepare my unique dishes. When everyone left, I walked Lucy back home again, but then we decided to return to my house.

After we quickly cleaned everything up, we went upstairs and settled on the couch, looking at the shining Christmas tree.

"You know, I want already have my own home, incarnate my dreams, first, second, third. All the other little things, like my favorite salad, remind me of the New Year. O remember that every day, like a New Year, and I'm glad to spend it with you".

She touched my lips with her, then gently and carefully licked with her tongue over my lips. We again slightly moved each other mouths.

- Well, what if I kiss you? "I whisper, as if afraid to frighten her away.

- "It's driving me insane, very interesting for me because I'm sure you do it very well, but it will mean something more than just a kiss or experiment. I do not want you and me to be hurt, because I think I see what your eyes are trying to tell me. Nevertheless, this will mean that you give your heart to me. I give you mine, and we must protect them and never hurt, be honest and faithful in their feelings. And this should be forever. If it is not so, then it is better to stop now because, in my opinion, we went too far already. Some people have started to notice it".

I did not say anything but just continued to look into her eyes for a few more seconds. Then we tied the agreement of our hearts with a kiss.

Next day I bade farewell to her at the train station. After all, my friends and I began to prepare for the New Year. But I could not think of anything except her. My heart was beating so hard. I fell in love with it. On New Year's Eve, I could not get through the lines to call her. I did not know what to think.

On the next morning, I got a text saying that she is going back tonight, although she had to return onlyin a week. My joy knew no bounds. I did not want to let her go anymore, no more than a meterfrom me. The next month it was the way it was. We spent all our days together and, of course, with our friends. We celebrated Christmas together and rode with mummers to the parents of friends, sang and had fun. It seemed that this life would not end; we were together. Her hand held mine.

She was saying how she feels too; we were telling it to each other when we were alone. We continued having extended conversations. I could not get enough of her eyes, just as her smile, radiant with joy.

It seemed that I was the happiest, and I did not need anyone else in this life.

"You know, falling in love lasts three or four months, and if that time passes. You feel the same; then you love this person. While we are still at the stage of falling in love".

I took her hand, "And I know that I love you. You always tell me what you think so that I could answer. Please don't be silent".

"You see; I already broke my heart once; it was not so long ago. It turned out that he was playing with my feelings. He did not love me. Just promise me that you will not ask me about this person.

You will not seek him or spend your time on him. He was older than me by five years. I decided that he chose me and wants to live his whole life with me, at least, he said so. I skipped lectures, spending with him all the time. Even at work helping him, we lived together. But one day he just said that I do not fit him. "I'm sorry that I wasted your time…" He turned out to be such a hypocrite. I was just a toy for him, full of energy and enthusiasm, and he was tired of it. Hysteria happened to me. I began to push and insult him. Un the end, he could not restrain himself and hit me in the chest with his fist".

"Sunny, I'm sorry! Damn, something is piercing my heart".

"Maybe you'll have a pill?"

"Even in my childhood, my heart took hold of me, but I was told that it just needs to grow."

- "You did not promise me something."

"It's hard to describe my feelings right now," I walked away and leaned on the stand, "You'd better not tell me this. It hurts me that someone hurt you".

"Sasha, please, promise."

"Ok, I promise."

She came to me. I gave her a tight hug; I saw the pain in her eyes from these memories.

"I do not want to let you go anywhere so that no one else will hurt you. Did I say it out loud?"

"Yes," she smiled and kissed me on the neck, " William, the phone is ringing. Can you pick up the phone?"

"Hello, Mom. It's all right; I wanted to ask you something! What if I celebrate my birthday on the twentieth and not the twenty-first of January, do you come twenty-second in the morning?"

"Dad says that when we arrive, then you will celebrate! And you cannot rejoice in advance. It's bad luck".

"All right."

"Okay, we have to go to the gym in the evening we'll call again."

"Sasha, darling, do you have a birthday twenty-first?"

"Yes, but I decided to celebrate in twentieth."

"Maybe you should listen to your parents?"

"I just wanted to be at home with you and with friends. Then again with my parents."

'As you know,'.

"Congratulations! "My friends screaming were coming into the house with sparkling lights in their hands and some bubbles. Everything was hilarious. We summed up all the unforgettable moments of the winter break. Our party ended almost in the morning. I was about to escort Lucy back home as someone rang the doorbell. I have decided that one of the friends forgot something. I opened the door.

"Surprise, happy birthday! "Mom and Dad stood in the doorway.

"Hi! Have you just changed the tickets?"

"No, they were initially on the twenty-first."

"Are you tipsy? We have forbidden to celebrate in advance".

"I did not observe it in advance. I was congratulated at midnight. I'll be right back!"

I urgently needed to get Lucy out of the house while my parents were bringing their suitcases. We ran to another veranda. I opened the window and gently put her down from the first floor through the window. Which was relatively high about her.

"Will not you be afraid to get home yourself?"

"No."

"Call me when you're at home. I'm sorry that it happened!"

"I told you he would not listen. Sasha, what is it?"

"Mom, I'll clean it up myself!"

"Yeah! You celebrated to glory, I'll have a look to cellar tomorrow, so I will not be distraught today."

"Dad, I took only a little bit of win. We had guests, and mom said that I could. I don't understand why you are so angry".

"Because you did not listen:

"I went to bed tomorrow morning I'll clean it all if you want to eat. There's a lot of food in the fridge".

Mom went upstairs to my room.

"William, tell me honestly, you did not take any drugs?"

"In terms of what? Of course, not. What kind of questions is that?"

- "Well, it's just that you had such strange eyes."

"Do not tell me anything. Do not talk about it! How could you think such a thing?"

"Okay, okay. Tell me, was Lucy here, too?

"Yes, why?"

"Well, we know that you spent the whole Christmas together."

"How do you?"

"The rumor you pick up on the streets."

"All right. I'm so tired of it".

"Okay, son, good night!".

Once again, the school began. Our team began to prepare for a new basketball season. Often I returned home later than usual because I was seeing Lucy. We decided to leave everything as it is. Do not say anything to my parents, although they understood everything themselves.

We won the game after game. My main viewer was on the podium, which made me think that my forces were unlimited. And in the end I decided that everything can be adjusted, you need to talk to your parents, they must understand.

And everything seems to be going well, Lucy and I were engaged in a project in which we had to win. It was an annual match in humor and acting between all the educational institutions of our small town. Most of whose inhabitants came to look at us in the central house of culture. The Director was very worried since us winning determined the reputation of the Lyceum. We had to perform at the proper level. Lucy was the leader. We, trained on Saturday nights in the actor's games, we're 100% ready. Since we invented our acts and every-everything our, unlike others - everything was stolen from the Internet. This shameful, nothing good wearing Russian show - "Comedy club," to which everyone was so imitated. The judges unanimously announced our victory, many parents who were in the hall rose and clapped for us. It was our triumph but among the guests. I, as always, did not find my parents whom I so hoped to see. We went on stage, holding hands. There were all my friends and of course, Lucy, without which nothing would happen, and bowed as befits.

Another victory, but the main match for our basketball team was ahead, the final game, as well as one more competition.

I returned home and happily tell about how everything was terrific, having decided to talk with my mother and about more pressing.

"Yes, Sash, I also want to talk to you. Not that I'm against it, but I think you should stop seeing Lucy.

How much older is she, five or six years?"

"What's the difference, what age? I will not stop anything. I know what to do myself. How can you even influence this? This is mine and only my life".

"I forbid you! You know that her parents are divorced, but still live in together.

"You cannot forbid me anything. I did not know it, but it does not change anything for me".

I got up and left. It was already evening when I decided to see Lucy.

"Do not take everything close to heart. Do not think anything wrong, Okay?"

"What happened? You're shaking".

"Mom is against the fact that we are together!"

"She said that. Did she not explain why she was against it?"

"Because 'you do not suit me." You are older, and your parents are divorced, but still live together. Overall, all this has nothing to do with you and me. I'll calm down and talk to her; everything will be fine. Do you hear me?"

"I do not know, Willy."

"I'll figure it out. I'll explain who you are. Mom loves me very much. She will understand everything. I think she just been told some gossip, but do not worry, we'll fix it."

"All right, let's wait."

We sat and talked for a long time.

"I'll have to go to Kiev for a couple of days."

"Well, that's fine, I'll deal with this little problem."

Then I did not yet know what would happen in the next couple of days. It turned out that my mother was walking along the corridor and met Lucy's mother. She stated that she thinks that her daughter was suitable for me and that we should solve this by ourselves.

"That's exactly how she said?"

"Yes, exactly like this. Imagine how uncomfortable I was. I had to apologize for that. And it's not that I had to apologize! We talked about this only with you. You went and immediately said everything to her".

"Mom, we did not negotiate. You ordered me".

"What we talk about in the family should remain in the family and not go beyond it. How can I now look into the eyes of Lucy's mother? We see each other almost every day at work? You decided that you are an adult, but you do not think yet about your words. Which can lead to different consequences, and not only in this case but also for your father? He has to meet her at work too. You do not understand what you did".

"And what, do you want me to go and make one's living by myself to prove that I'm an adult?"

"You do not listen to us at all."

"I understood everything."

"Oh, I cannot deal with it anymore. I need water. Matthew talks to him".

"Son, I tell you as your father, I raised you. I am sure that better for you is to study. All these are your games, although you decided that you are already an adult, and you can earn money yourself. But I can tell you for sure that this is not as simple as it seems to you. Talking about Lucy, soon she will want to have a child. You're not even going to have a diploma. How are you going to support your family? Consider that right now; you are blocking yourself all opportunities in life.

Listen to me; soon you will go to university, another life will begin there. You will have a bunch of other girls, so do not spoil everything now. If you are an adult, then you will understand this, so let's finish it all. Mom cannot worry so much, but you just stitched her up".

"I know, Dad. You're right. I'll do it all, but I need a little time. Mom, do not worry; everything will be fine; I understood everything. I will fix everything. I will not take anything beyond the circle of the family. I will finish it all".

"We only want the best for you."

"I understand everything! I'll prepare for the lessons".

My heart was broken and compressed with pain. I turned my back to my parents to go into the room, as tears streamed from my eyes. Although I did not utter a sound or wipe them. My soul was crying because I betrayed it. I revealed love, betrayed everything that I believed in, because I really felt, really loved. I just knew it, like the fact that now, after giving up and stopping to fight. I surrendered, just surrendered, and only betrayed.

"I betrayed you! So I told you about the conversation with my parents, but this time do not say anything to your mother. Please! Let's not talk about anything at all; let's continue to be together.

When the moment comes, we will start our new life. We will declare it everyone and we'll not need to ask for permission".

"But William, I think, your parents are right."

"In terms of what?"

"You need to study; this is important. But I agree with your plan; we may as well check our feelings. I have a little news for you, too. In a month I'm leaving to study in Germany, I was given a visa".

"How?"

"You know, I'm already have done so much here, it's time to leave. I'll stay for one more month. I need to prepare for my studies, but I will not teach at the Lyceum anymore".

"I need to think it over."

"I've missed you."

"I do too. You know, my mom says that everything that happened for the best".

"Maybe this is precisely what we need."

I do not know if, at that moment of our conversation, she felt my hesitations because I could not say that I had agreed. I felt like that this could be the end.

The whole next month we spent together, knowing that we will get a part for a long time.

"William, I have another question," She narrowed her eyes and squeezed her lips not to laugh, "What will you do when I get fat, and I will have wrinkles?"

"Well, firstly, you are wonderful, and seeing your mother, I do not think that you will be plump."

"And what about Dad?"

"But if it happens, I'll just buy a bigger bed."

"This is what I love you for."

"And I love you for everything because you are in my life. Because you were in my life. I said to myself in thought, from which my heart was torn."

"Dad sent a text that he will be in five minutes near the monument to the dead soldiers. I need to go, because he, as always in a hurry and will leave without me. I wanted to talk to him."

"Maybe in the evening, will you see me?"

"Of course, my love, I already miss you. I have not even left yet! By the way, guys take offense at me, that I do not spend time with them anymore. They called me to hang out today; today is Saturday."

"Do you want to go?"

"I want you. I want to see you! See you later, my dear."

I ran to the monument, and for the first time in a long time, my father was already waiting for me.

Not the other way around, as it usually was.

"Are you still seeing her? I ask, are you still seeing her?"

"Dad, it's okay, she leaves to Germany in a week," I sighed heavily, "To study, and that's it."

"Well, I hope so."

"How can it be otherwise?"

This morning I woke up later than usual, even it was the middle of the week. I ran to Lucy through our place. There was no snow already for a long time only puddles and a half-green grass around.

I entered the apartment and saw the prepared luggage by the door. We still had half an hour, which we spent very quiet, almost in silence. The taxi pulled up earlier. As always, I opened the door and holding Lucy's hand put her in the back seat. I walked around the car and sat on the other side. I held her tender hand and looked at her, but she could not look at me. I saw a tear dripping down her cheek.

I wiped it and kissed her on the cheek. She began to cry even more. Lucy took a deep breath, got herself together, and wiped away her tears. We have already arrived at the bus station. The driver unloaded the luggage.

"I do not want to let you go."

"I do not make you promise me anything, but for this time, my heart is in your hands. When you fall out of love or decide that this is all, say it right away." It hurts me to say these words.

"You've already said everything. This is the only time I have nothing to say. I want so much to say and do. I love you. You will always be in my heart."

It was our farewell kiss. Our hands opened, but our fingers still wanted to reach each other out.

My lips were so salty, and throats could not swallow saliva. I was already biting the cheekbones from the fact that we parted. We did not know what would happen further, but from now on I started dreaming about the day when we will meet again.

Only a week later, I received the first e-mail. Rhen another in a couple of weeks, where she wrote that she had a hectic life out there and did not have time, but she liked it. Sometimes I called her on international lines, which was not very pleasant for my parents when they got a phone bill. My life went on. I worked hard and continued to study. I rearrange my room. I began spending more time with my friends.

One evening a bell rang:

"Hi, dear," A voice whispered.

"Lucy? Does something happen?"

"I have a little problem here. Please contact my mother to call my lawyer, let him come over. He's here, on the in the town, but I lost his number. I'll explain everything to you, do not worry, do it, as I ask".

I have never felt at ease. I called her mom and passed everything. But these three days turn out to be the most painful in my life. But at last, I received a letter in which Lucy wrote:

She lived with a family, husband, wife, and child. The husband began to annoy her, and when she refused him, he complained to his wife that Lucy annoys him. They need to do something. His wife's reaction was adequate; she called the police. But the lawyer came and settled everything. So now everything is fine. She lives in another house with another family. Thank you for helping. I miss you.

Parents, of course, saw my condition and believed that she did not protect me if she made me be so.

Time passed, our lives became too different, and the distance was excruciating torture. The end of the school year. It was already warm outside when I was sitting at the stadium after training and typing a farewell letter. It was the end; my heart was suffering too much. I understood that this couldn't continue, even I still loved her but decided to let her go because I did not see our future together.

I made this decision and even informed everyone about it. that again I became no one; I hated myself and everything around.

What I did and how I felt overwhelmed me. When I went out of the game, I could not concentrate.

I played rough. I was put on the bench. I decided that I should start seriously doing soccer and a a lot of training.

At the next training session, we are finally playing with each other. So I see how I run with the ball running to the gate, and only for a second. I was distracted to look at the place where Lucy would be sitting. Today she was not there; she was gone. I'm SUCH an ASSHOLE! Suddenly, in front of me, appears a defender who doesn't move. I decide to go to the right, but my left leg was not in the right position. I turn my foot; my gaze instantly appears to be looking down. Where I see the sole of my foot from above. A terrible pain pierced me, and I fell, sharply screaming. I broke down. I'm broken. I was dragged to the bike of my friend David drove me home.

Gradually, life began to improve. I studied at home, lying in a cast. I used my father's old car, or rather his first car, which he gave it to me. Three months later, I had passed all the exams ahead of time with an "excellent," took off the cast right before the Promenade dance.

I returned to the joy of the life of friends and parents. Everyone around was satisfied, everyone but me. Next preparation for the university and, of course, graduation. Photos in the album, where we all standing as one, graduation. Where I felt so alone, but certainly did not show it.

With my heart and mind, I have a newfound self-awareness.

Is our one existence that will lead to imminent death? Will the planet on which we live soon die? In the modern world, it is necessary for one to question everything, to understand how to live and survive.

Polish King Borislav in 1117 attacked a weakened Russia and decided to conquer and annex the country until the beginning of the 15th century. Hus, the western part of the former Rus was under tyranny and in the enslavement of the Polish Lithuanian Commonwealth (modern day Poland).

The central-southern and eastern lands of Rus were devastated after the invasion of the Mongol-Tatars.

From all over Rus, those who never will tolerate slavery from dictators and power, not pure and soul labial gather and run away to these lands. Tsar Rus in Ukraine already unable to keep promises to the Rus people. The Muscovites had to put up with the illegitimate Tsar of Rus who soon would be replaced with the even more illegitimate royal family. On the territory of Crimea, the power of fear and slavery with robbery suited the Crimean Khanate which, like the Moscow kingdom in the collapse of the Mongol-Tatar yoke. They received the same independence from the Ottoman Empire after the collapse of the Golden Horde.

These times were full of suffering for the Rusichs, so they began to return to their native land and go to the area where everyone who wants to save the right word and soul gathers, gathered in dozens - "Sichs."

To save the life of Rusich, as one nation. Throughout the former territory of Russia, a rumor spread about how the people are going to protect themselves from enemies, that they were from all sides and that they wanted to destroy and enslave them.

In the sovereign territories of the "wild field" Sichs began to form, one after another growing into well-fortified fortresses.

The main conditions for getting into the Sich were:

1. Knowledge of the Ukrainian language, only this way it was possible to expose the spy from the Muscovites or the Poles. Since in all the other methods, they were very similar to the Rusics.

2. Confess to the Orthodox faith.

3. Pass military training.

4. Obey the rules of the main Sich established by Ataman, who was the commander-in-chief over all his people. He was chosen for courage and wisdom. Murder in Sich was punishable by the death penalty, as well as stealing, deception, and exceptionally brutal drunkenness.

Since those people considered themselves free and independent. They called themselves Cossacks and Ukrainians because they spoke correctly in the Ukrainian language, not in Polish or Muscovite.

This is how the long path of Ukraine in the struggle for independence, freedom of will, and speech began.

1621 - Turkish Sultan Osman II collected 22000 troops and along with thousands of his Crimean vassals moved to Pospolita. 40,000a strong army of Cossacks with the face of Hetman rescued Poland and maybe all Europe from imminent death.

First time name of Peter Sahaidachny - the leader of the Cossacks became known in 1606. Petro Konashevych- Sahaidachny drove the Cossacks to successful campaigns in the Crimea and Turkey. He captured the fort of Varna. Under his command, the troops of Zaporozhye in the Polish army almost succeeded in destroying Moscow, only Sahaidachny's mistakes stopped the offensive that was in full swing. It was his talent as a commander that saved Central Europe from the invasion of the Ottoman Empire in 1621. After the cruel defeat at Tsetsera, the Polish King appealed to the Cossacks for military assistance. He invited the Sahaidachny to Warsaw. They showed him great respect, and the King himself spooked to Sahaidachny with the words: "I send my son to Khotyn and entrust his life to You". At the call of King Sigismund III under Khotyn, 40,000 Cossacks gathered. Under the leadership of the HHetman's King Jan Karl Hotkevich, 35,000 Polyakov and 25,000 Lithuanians who were opposed to the 220,000 wars of the Ismanskaya Empire.

The Khotyn battle began on September 2 by the offensive of the leading forces on all fronts and a concentrated blow to the central regiments of the Cossacks Petro Sahaidachny. At night, Hetman ordered to the Cossacks to build (unusual at this time) structures of a dug-out type. Which allowed them to withstand a constant shelling from cannons, which lasted more than five hours.

After the artillery went in the infantry. Sahaidachny saw this and ordered to be built on three lines and shooting in the first row led a constant fire with rifles which they actively recharged and changed for volley fire from the next row. Sahaidachny also ordered during the Janissary attack to regroup on the flanks. They surround the enemy by increasing the area of shelling on the enemy who was tearing at the center of the Zaporozhye army through a previously disguised, excavated ditch. Turks hastily retreating lost about 10 thousand troops.

September 23

"I will not eat or drink until you bring Sahaidachny," angrily ordered the Sultan of the Ottoman Empire.

Meanwhile, the southern side of the defense of the Ottoman Empire did not expect the next morning raid, led by Petro Konashevych-Sahaidachny.

With the sound of a saber and gunshot, every man rushed to fight in the Osman camp. Immediately a servant flew into the tent and shouted fiercely that Sahaidachny with the Cossacks were here and that they were breaking through the defenses!

All those who could, irrespective of the rank, were already running, that there were forces. Then Osman ordered to everybody to assemble hastily, but before that, he gave the order to select personal mercenaries. That when Sahaidachny rushes closer, they shoot him with poisoned arrows.

The Hetman had an excellent horse, and he was as an example to everyone on that horse, but one arrow still got him in the battle.

The French historian Bodie: "With such boldness the Cossacks pursued the Turks, sweeping away everything in their path, which almost broke through to the banners and hints of the Sultan himself."

The Armenian chronicler wrote: "If it were not for the Cossacks, the Polish army would have been broken down in three days. The victory was achieved only by the help of God and the Cossacks."

Petro Konashevych-Sahaidachny died on June 20, 1622, in the city of Kiev.

Before his death as a reward from the hands of King Vladislav for his successful actions under the Khotyn Fortress. He received a sword encrusted with gold and diamonds.

There is an inscription in Latin: "Vladislav grateful to Kontsevich, for a fight under Khotin against Osman."

So one of the most respected rulers of central Europe recognized the great achievements of the Cossacks in defense of Ukraine, Pospolita and other countries from the Turkish danger.

How It would not be strange, but after all these, Kazakov and the whole Ukraine tried to enslave. The Polish gentry wanted more and more power. The rebels were suppressed with the help of the army, like with Kosinsky, and often they insidiously were killing. That also happened to Ivan Sulim Hetman of the Zaporozhye army.

Ten years later, "It was awful for me to live in Cherkassy, that one in all Ukraine. The Szlachta, the law after the law and their faith, are planted. Even the soul asks to play on the kobza, "Said Father Szlachta (from the High German Slacht (modern German Geschlecht) gender, breed, sex) a privileged estate in the societies of the middle and contemporary times, in a broader sense - military-served nobility or clan aristocracy.

Kobza is a Ukrainian lute-like stringed plucked musical instrument with 4 (and more) twin strings.

"Ukraine is in the world right now. The land is fertile, in every yard, you can find a cow, piglets, birds. All bazaars full of everything you may need, everybody educated, no need to go to study abroad in Germany or Poland. In Kiev, science is just as strong as it used to be after Russia. When were we living so last time? Ukraine blooms", said, mother "Let me wash my hands, then I'll answer you. They're as black as night."

"We should have supper. The son came from the long road, came to us before even seeing the Vinnytsia."

Vinnytsia is a city on the Southern Bug River, in west-central Ukraine.

"Ukrainians are not allowed to sell their goods in the markets. The fact that all the smart and do not want to fight. Namely, this youth is one hope. After all, for how long a clever society can live under someone else's power having such a history in the past that is transmitted by the truth from the mouth of the father to his son. So it was and will always be in every family in Ukraine."

Father replied "For years of peace, I am giving up on and would not have enough power even to fight, other ways I would…"

He looked at his son. The son looked at his father. They both smiled. "The Slacht completely unbuttoned" "God sees everything."

"Let's sit outside the house under the viburnum. Oh, how the nightingale chirps. Do you hear that?"

"Per for many years the world is in the peace, that's our son has already grown. And so, it will," said the mother.

Ivan stood by the window, looked menacingly. Wide-shoulders, straight back, his hands are folded.

Nearly rebelled at the words of his mother. He struck the windowsill and left the house.

"Do not break the house. You did not build it," said father smilingly.

"Oksana carried everything where you said, "replied the mother "You learned science. I see you have become a strong man, but do you think in spirit. Are you ready to fight for the whole honor and the truth of Rusich, for Ukraine?"

"Ready? I learned everything. I learned all my feelings and mind, how to use my saber so that I can be worthy Cossack. A knight. Came to say goodbye, January to me, Mom will become. The Dnepr father, we will not see each other more." Said, Ivan

"Where are you going son? You've just arrived; you're too young to fight yet, what if you get killed?" said the mother, anxiously.

"Well done, son. I did not think that you would be a good person because of your character and disobedience in childhood," Congratulated the father.

"I came to you ask for a blessing. It will save me if it is your will to give it to me, "said the son.

The mother ran into the house and instantly returned. She unfolded a bundle with icons and embroidery.

Tear-stained torrents streamed from her. She could not utter a word from her mouth. Ivan got down on his knee and bowed to his parents. The father laid his hands on his head and read a prayer in his voice, "Take care of yourself, son, and even more importantly, take care of Ukraine." Ivan got up and kissed his mother and father. He hugged them with mightily in his arms, then jumped on his horse and prepared to ride off into the field.

"Son, take my kobza, play on it at the bad times and everything with you will be well. This means you and Ukraine," said his father.

"Thank you, father, "said his son.

Ivan smiled, tears started welling. He waved it with his hand, unfolded the horse bravely. He galloped away.

They stood and looked after their son, the night became bright, and for a long time they could see Ivan galloping under the sky along the Milky Way.

That's where is the first thing.

Khmelnytsky was born in the village of Subotiv, near Chyhyryn in the Crown of the Kingdom of Poland at the estate of his father, Mykhailo Khmelnytsky. His father, a courtier of Great Crown Hetman Stanisław Żółkiewski was of noble birth and belonged to the Clan Massalski, Abdank or Syrokomla, but there had been controversy as to whether Bohdan belonged to the szlachta (the Polish term for noblemen). Some sources state that in 1590 his father Mykhailo was appointed as a sotnyk for the Korsun-Chyhyryn starosta Jan Daniłowicz, who continued to colonize the new Ukrainian lands near the Dnieper river. According to the above-mentioned-source, Mykhailo established Chyhyryn and later his family estates of Subotiv (5 miles from Chyhyryn) and Novoseltsi. Khmelnytsky identified as a noble, and his father's status as a deputy Starosta (elder) of Chyhyryn helped him to be considered as such by others. During the uprising, however, Khmelnytsky would stress his mother's Cossack roots and his father's exploits with the Cossacks of the Sich.

Upon completion of his studies in 1617, Khmelnytsky entered into service with the Cossacks. As early as 1619 he was sent together with his father to Moldavia when the Polish–Lithuanian Commonwealth entered into war against the Ottoman Empire. His first military engagement was a tragic one. During the battle of Cecora (Ţuţora) on September 17, 1620, his father was killed. A young Khmelnytsky, among many others including future hetman Stanisław Koniecpolski, was captured by the Turks. He spent the next two years in captivity in Constantinople as a prisoner of an Ottoman Kapudan Pasha (presumably Parlak Mustafa Pasha). Other sources claim that he spent his slavery in Ottoman Navy on galleys as an oarsman, where he picked up a knowledge of Turkic languages.

Later Bohdan Khmelnytsky married Hanna Somkivna, a daughter of a rich Pereyaslavl Cossack; the the couple settled in Subotiv.

After the death of the Polish King Sigismund III in April 1632, the Cossack sergeant sent his representatives to the Seim with a demand to allow participation in the election of a new king and to weaken national and religious oppression.

The Seim of Rzeczpospolita is a caste-representative body in the Commonwealth in the second half of the 16th - 18th centuries.

On provincial meeting in Ukraine, the question of the needs to return to Orthodox believers their rights, which they are deprived after the conclusion of the Brest Union.

Mogila was supported by the Lithuanian Hetman, King Christopher Radziwill. At the convective meeting in Warsaw, Orthodox and Protestants put together their demands formulated at 14 points.

According to this document, the Orthodox Church in Ukraine officially received the right to have its hierarchy headed by the metropolitan and four bishops (Lviv, Lutsk, Peremyshl, Mstislavsky), free to send service, have churches, monasteries, print shops, schools, brotherhoods.

Orthodox churches were returned to churches and monasteries in Kiev.

For everything else, however, the courts in the localities would issue all decisions in the direction of the Polish Szlyachta. The Jews, whom Kozaks are asked in the document to the King to expel from Ukraine.

For a long time, officials of the Commonwealth of Pospolite in Ukraine, political opponents of King Vladislav IV watched Ukraine with skepticism.

The Polish gentry was particularly hostile to Bogdan Khmelnitsky, a supporter of Vladislav IV and one of the carriers of autonomist views. Chyhyryn - Konetspolsky: crowned HHetman Stanislav and his son, the coroner Alexander with the help of his Chigirinsky elder D. Chaplinsky.

In total Khmelnitsky had ten children. He took advantage of the absence of Polish elder Chaplinsky, who hated Khmelnytsky and attacked his farm, plundering it. They took his wife Elena, with whom Khmelnytsky had lived with after the death of his first wife. He married to her by Catholic rite and beat the youngest son of Khmelnytsky to death.

Khmelnytsky rose up in spirit and flesh against the Polish Szlachta in Ukraine.

In early February 1648, a group of Cossacks with Khmelnitsky arrived in Zaporozhye. The departure did not arouse any suspicion thoughts from the local administration, since it was a regular event.

Gathered Zaporozhs around him on Tomakovka Island, which was down along the Dnieper River 60 km south of Khortitsa Island. Khmelnitsky decided to go to Sich, located on the Nikitsky Horn.

On the Sich since 1638 there was a garrison of the Crown troops. The detachment of Khmelnitsky defeated the Polish garrison and gathered all power to Poland.

First, the newly elected Hetman Bogdan Khmelnitsky took the following steps:

• Sent universals to the Ukrainian people with appeals to join the ranks of the Cossack army.

• Established the production of gunpowder, organized the purchase of weapons and ammunition.

• Named four famous Cossacks as their closest associates and commanders. One of which was Colonel Ivan Bohun, who courageously showed himself and rose to his rank. Ivan Bohun, despite his popularity and mind among the Cossacks, could himself be a Hetman, but this is the rare case that shows a person putting his interests below the interests of the Cossacks, Russian (Rusich), and Ukraine.

• Enlisting the support of the Ottoman Empire, in February-March 1648 in Bakhchisaray, Ukrainian ambassadors agreed with the Crimean Khan Islam-Grey on military assistance in the war against the Polish.

This was the beginning of a new wave of the armed fight for the equality of rights of Ukraine and Pospolita.

The Battle of Yellow Waters

After waiting for the 3-4 thousand man-strong armies of Perekop Murza at the end of April the 8, thousandth registered Cossack army withdrew from the Sich. Nikolai Pototsky sent four regiments of Cossacks in boats down the Dnieper. Two more attached to the "quartz" detachment, which came from Krylov to meet the insurgents. The general management of these troops numbering 5-6 thousand people, supposed to carry out the 20-year-old son of Nikolai Stepan Pototsky. Both the HHetman the coroner Nikolai Pototsky and the Polar Martin Kalinovsky remained in the camp between Cherkassy and Korsun while waiting for reinforcements. On April 22, 1648, the four thousand strong armies of Khmelnitsky stepped out of Zaporizhia. Behind him at a distance was Tugai-bey with three thousand Tatars. After passing the fortress Kodak, where the Polish garrison was sitting, Khmelnytsky went to the mouth of the river Tasmin and stopped camp on the tributary Yellow Waters, converge into Tasmin (in the present Dnepropetrovsk region). A few days later, under the command of the young Stefan

Potocki, the Poles, also approached only five thousand men and eight cannons. Poles were waiting for reinforcements from two regiments of Cossacks who descended by boat along the river.

The Dnieper, but they bit their commanders and went over to Khmelnytsky faster; a truce was signed, and the Poles gave Khmelnitsky artillery in exchange for the hostages, Colonels Mikhail Rat and Maxim Krivonos.

Then the Cossacks conducted a deceptive attack on the camp of the Poles and the hostage Cossack colonels demanded horses to stop the "offensive." As soon as they were given horses, they galloped to the insurgents to "stop them." Instead, they fled. After Khmelnitsky took over artillery, the position of the Polish army became hopeless. The Poles tried to convey information about their difficult situation to the main army, which was near Korsun, in many ways: even an attempt was made to transmit a note with a specially trained dog. But all efforts were fruitless. After the transfer of the Cossacks to the side of Khmelnytsky, the Polish army had a "shortage" in the infantry and could not defend itself. May 5, after several Tatar-Cossack attacks on the camp, it was decided to retreat, fenced off with rows of wagons from the flanks. But near the tract Knyazhie Bayraki in the upper reaches of the Dneprovoy Kamenka river, an ambush was made by the Cossacks and Tatars. The way of retreat was dug in trenches, and the retreating Poles were utterly routed. Stepan Pototsky was mortally wounded, other chiefs were taken as a war prisoner and sent captives to Chigirin.

It was then that the siege of Lviv and Zamoschem was carried out, a vast territory of Ukraine was liberated from the power of Pospolita. Participant events, Protector R. Shell, describes this wave of the revolution, which began in 1648 and reached its peak next year:

"Yes, everything alive has risen to the Cossacks, until hardly knew in which village such a person. If he could not go himself, the son to go to the troops. If he was unwell, then the servant boy was sent, and some of them were from the courtyard, only one was found, and it was difficult to hire. Slander was in the cities there were also the rights of the Maideborsk and Burmistrov advisers, and the assessors left their ranks. They shaved their beards, and so the troops marched on."

On the second day of the new year, 1649 Khmelnitsky triumphantly drove through the Golden Gate to Kiev, who welcomed him with church chimes, cannon shots and thousands of people. Students of the Kiev Academy welcomed him with recitations like Moses, God's prophet. He was a liberator from the Polish captivity of the Orthodox population.

He was welcomed by Patriarch Pavis of Jerusalem and Metropolitan of Kiev Sylvester Kossov. A few days later, the Patriarch at Sofievsky Cathedral dismissed all present and future sins and in absentia married the HHetman with Motren (Elena Chaplinskaya). The Patriarch blessed him with cannon shots for the war with the Poles,

"The luminous possessor and King of Russia" with the highest Orthodox clergy, the Kiev intelligentsia and the Patriarch of Jerusalem, Paisiustestified that the beginning of the new Cossack-hetman state, Khmelnytsky's proper state was made. The Patriarch of sanctified the decision of B. Khmelnitsky to fight against the oppressorsConstantinople (Ioannicius II or Parthenius II) in 1651. Sent by the Corinthian metropolitan with a sword consecrated on the coffin of the Lord, which the HHetman banded around him". [31]

Negotiations, begun in Zamosc, continued in Kiev in early 1649. Before the negotiating commission appeared "new" Khmelnitsky:

The truth is existing, saying discouraged to ambassadors. That I am a small man, insignificant person, but God gave me this, and now I am the sole owner and autocrat of Russia. I will beat out the entire Rus people from the Lyadsky captivity. That earlier, I fought for my harm and untruth, then from now on, I will fight for our Orthodox faith. Renounce the Poles and stay with the Cossacks, because the Lyadsky land will rot, and Russia will reign. I am freely in control of my Kiev. I am the master and governor of Kiev; God gave me this with the help of my saber.

From the journal of the Polish embassy you can see how Khmelnitsky quickly turned from a supporter of the "Cossack autonomy" in the lands of the Nadniprovschina to the liberator from Polish captivity of the whole Russian, now Ukrainian, people between Lvov, Holm, and Galich.

Khmelnytsky understood that for the success of the uprising, he needed a foreign ally, that in other words it was at the same time recognition of the power of such an international state.

A convenient ally could be the Turkish Sultan, but dislike of the Cossacks' to basurmans made Bogdan, an alliance against Poland and the weakened Kingdom of the Moscow unacceptable. Just after the war with Poland, to take Hetman and his one of the most skilled and active Zaporozhian troops under his arm. On December 31, 1653, the Kingdom of Moscow and the Hetman Ukraine declared war on the Rech Pospolitaya.

In 1654 at the Pereyaslavka Rada, it was decided to make Ukraine the jurisdiction of the Moscow State, while retaining all the rights and liberties of the Zaporozhye army and could negotiate with everybody, the Tatars and Polish recorded all this in their articles.

In the spring the Tsar with the army went to Lithuania and quickly captured Mogilev, Polovsk, Smolensk, Minsk, Vilna. At the same time, Swedish King Charles X attacked Warsaw. Krakow, and Khmelnytsky recaptured Galich and Volhyn, defeating the Polish army under "City" and overlaid the city of Lviv. Poland was on the edge of defeat. King Jan Kazimir fled to Selezia from where he asked Khmelnitsky twice not to allow the destruction of the Polish-Lithuanian Commonwealth. The old HHetman replied:

"Let Poland abandon everything that belonged to the ancient kingdoms of the Russian land, return whole Russia to Cossacks including Vladimir, Lvov, Yaroslav, Przemysl and formally proclaim it free.

Then we will live with Poland, as neighbors and friends, and not as slaves and subjects. We will sign peace on eternal tablets as soon as it's done, but this will not happen while in Poland there are Szlachta, there will be no peace between Russians and Poles.

Bogdan Zinovy Mikhaylovich Khmelnitsky died August 6, 1657, not knowing that before his death Ukraine was signed into allies.

Ivan Bohun still fought with the Poles and was in another campaign, burned half of the Rech Pospolitaya, despite the decree of Khmelnytsky. The agreement between Mosua and the King of Poland, when he got the news of the death of the great Hetman.

Returning from Poland Ivan Bohun got on the crossing the river. With him in the boat was a blind kobza player and a little boy on the raft.

"What are you squinted Cossack?"

"Do you think kobza player does not know that when a Cossack sings, his soul is crying?"

"I see the Colonel, that the death of your friend is eating you and your heart indeed was stolen by Polish girl, rumors do not lie."

"Stole... I do not want to live anymore, inside everything is burned out like after a fire. I can't see any light through the pain of this. There is no light on this earth and will not be. It will not end, and we can't do anything about it, and it doesn't make sense anymore."

"Old, evil spirits ruined you Cossacks, but believe me, even her and all this, one more step towards victory of truth and good. It's well-known a long time ago."

"Where there is a chance to change our world, I'll change this eternal, and the world will finally be found in eternal glory and truth."

"So, it was with Elena Troyan; this happened with our God-given Ottoman and with you too. Women!

Then Elena was hanged before your battle, still, under Berestechkom, the son of Timos hung for treachery."

"Was she a traitor? I know that she loved him very much."

"Who knows how it is there. Maybe the Polish conceived it, or it was the truth..."

"So, it is with you. I know that pain in the heart; it's not what you destined and not what you need. You need a Ukrainian girl. You will only find real happiness with her and not because you are also a Ukrainian, it's just maybe not the right time yet. And how can she be yours, if the whole Poland, every man, and his dog is more afraid of us the devil. People built the towers to the sky. Do you think that our Lord has shown us in different tongues in vain?

And even now, if we speak the same language with our enemies from all sides, we still will not agree.

Until everyone decides to become the right person, and I believe such times will come, and we will all live by honor and truth. For which we are fighting in Ukraine and ourselves, you know it yourself."

Before women start defending their honor and master the culture of being the truth of life. The world will be in the agony of war. A man depends heavily on women and only what she allows he can get.

She can give the heart, or can only open her legs. You forgot, Colonel, your walk was too long, and in every place where you were, you will have roots. You must marry only one now, but still, serve only to the right cause - Ukraine of our Russia's mother, so soon the hours will come hard, that the devil's forces are all this land for her love for life and truth, and they will want to tear the fertile lands apart, so that all the hope on your sons."

"There is no truth in the world; Truth cannot be found,

What now is the lie, becomes truth,

Now the fact stands at the threshold,

And the mute lies sit at the end of the table.

Now the truth is trampled by feet,

And the wrong lie is treating with honey.

Now, truth sits at the dungeon,

And the lie in the light.

And already True weeping with tears,

And the lie still drinking and fooling around.

Where are you, True, did you died, or you are imprisoned,

Is the lie devoured the whole world?

Oh, who in the world will be True to make,

The Lord will bless this person,

Therefore, the Lord Himself is True and will rejuvenate pride,

He will crush the lie; he will pull up the holy things."

The Colonel thought over everything that had been said and sung by the Kobzar looking at the boundless, steppe, wheat fields on the clear-clear sky with the red-tinged veins-no place where there was such a heaven like that here in Russia. It was hard not to calm the soul because of all these thoughts.

The year 1651 - Polish troops ransacked every village Kazakov founded, stealing all the villagers and destroying all the churches and putting everything under fire.

Jan Kazimir and his lodged along with the combined forces from Europe came to the heart of that time Cossack power of Volhynia and stopped at Berestechko. On July 28, a professional Cossack army led by Colonel Ivan Bohun came to them.

The 105-thousand-strong Cossack army came under Berestechko; the regiments quickly settled down on advantageous positions. The primary detachment in the amount of 70 thousand Ivan Bogun placed on both sides of the road from Demeevka to Berestechko across the river on the opposite side of the village of Plyashev. The right flank of the camp is covered by the river Stir and the rear by river Plyashevka and the marshes. The left side is the 35,000 - active corps under the command of Danil Nychai from the back.

In the center, the Cossacks became well-protected by thieves and wagons. The next day comes hired army of Nogaev of the Crimean Tatars, 20,000 soldiers. Bogun favorably places them under the village of Korytny, where the enemy could not see them.

Thus, they would have to inflict an unexpected blow from the throat of the river and surround the enemy at the right time.

King Jan Kazimir following his plan went with the army to Rovno, but due to the troops of Ivan Bogun, he had to stop earlier.

The main camp (75 thousand, the artillery of 80 cannons, Germans, cavalry and 7 thousand dragoons) was located opposite the village of Berestechka, across the River Stir.

Dragoons (dragon, letter "dragon") is the name of the cavalry, capable of acting and on foot. In earlier times, this same name was understood as infantry, planted on horses.

The left flank, a little ahead, the king exposed the Swedish heavy cavalry 30 thousand. On the right side, Yarem Veshnevetsky with a body at 25 thousand infantries with 42 cannons. Further behind they have hidden a mounted regiment of hussars under the command of Pototsky.

The King waited several days for the Cossacks to attack and in the morning of the 2nd of August, the 35 thousandth Cossack cavalry under the command of Javan Sirk strikes an unexpected blow to the heavy Swedish cavalry. The shock was so rapid and intense that by noon, the enemy lost 17,000 of his soldiers and was forced to flee to the camp of the king. While the Cossacks were luckily occupied the left, already vulnerable flank of Jan Casimir. Ivan Bohun sent to everyone the most detailed plans for the attack of the next day. Suddenly the bribed Tatars left the battlefield. Khmelnitsky, according to some information, was captured when he tried to overtake them. According to another source, he craved for unanimity so much. That he was ready to sacrifice one defeat and part of the Cossacks and make a deal to kidnap him this seems right, as a loyal person to the Polish crown with Jan Kazmir.

One way or another, when he left the battlefield, he remembered Bogdag as Ivan Bohun, even though he was surrounded in the castle. He nevertheless gathered his strength and broke not only the round of the castle but also found themselves in a series of round-ups of Khmelnitsky himself with the army.

Although at the time people were deciding on Zaporozhye, who will own the mace now. Could not stop thinking.

The mace is a symbol of high power and phallus. The Celts are the weapon of Dagda and the symbol of it as the lord of life and death.

On the 3rd or 4th of August, Ivan Bohun considered a new plan. Jan Kazimir rejoiced that the forces have become smaller and begin active operations.

After collecting the whole troop, he sends them along the Stir river, bypassing the forces of Zaporozhye.

The goal is to cut off the path to retreat.

On the 5th of August Jan Kazimir gives an order to the artillery, and the Cossacks are forced to flee to the main camp.

On the 6th of August, by the law of the King, the artillery was placed closer to the enemy camps. One hundred twenty cannons launched a massive shelling of the Cossack troops.

The situation became strained; shelling did not stop for two days; a half thousand Cossacks were killed.

By the night of the second day, a crossing was made through which the Cossacks began to retreat to change the battlefield, on the orders of Ivan Bohun.

In the morning the troops withdrew to the road towards Plyashevka.

By four o'clock in the evening, the regiment of Nechai defended the retreat with 12 thousand brave soldiers. During this time, the Cossacks dug, another channel for the river Plyashevka was built to sweep downstream. Thereby raising the water level near the riverbed to create an island.

On the island were 300 characters and 70 volunteers, that would detain the army of the king.

These characters were warriors of a high military organization of precise field weapons.

For three days, Cossacks restrained the army of Jan Kazimir, who during this time lost about 4 thousand of their soldiers. All volunteers gave up their lives for the freedom of Ukraine and Orthodox faith, showing a great example of courage to all subsequent generations. The characters chanted since the first Cossack killed on the island "Eternal glory to heroes" or "Heroes do not die."

Teslugov, Kozin, Pitch, Verba by Kremenets, on the Stupne to Mizoch near Semidub, the 20 thousand regiments detained the king's army. For another day and so had to go on the road to disrepair and on August 13, leaving on the way Mirogosche, Mizoch.

For three days, Ivan Bohun distributed the troops in such a way that it would allow him to execute a convenient maneuver at any stage of the battle.

The main camp was in the valley under the mountain and was not visible to the enemy from either side. Two ambush regiments are located on both sides of the road near the village of Zalizzi; the army is well disguised. Reserve regiment of 35 thousand Cossacks is situated opposite the town of Urvena.

The artillery detachment is located in the forest and prepared for a targeted attack.

On August 17th, King Casimir led an army to the Mizoche district. On the same day, at noon, two ambush regiments under the command of Nichai and Radivila simultaneously beat the cavalry, which broke away two kilometers from the leading troops. Through the dense battle, cavalry detachments could not fight effectively. Artillery with the cannon fire forced the main forces to stop and leave the possibility of helping their cavalry. This battle was fierce and did not take prisoners. The 20 thousand-man army of one of the main colonels was defeated.

In the meantime, Ian Kazimir diverts the king's army from the shelling and builds them for the new start of the battle by dividing into three camps. Each on the flanks from the main army, in anticipation of being defended.

Colonel Ivan Bohun was not in a hurry to attack, forcing the army of Casimir to stand in the hot sun for five hours in a tense state.

Only in the evening Ivan Sirko, who was Bobrin's twin brother, left with five thousand troops of cavalry Cossacks and left just on the left flank. Earlier at the beginning of the battle, at the same time, Nichai's night attack was so swift that Vyshnevetsky's right side did not have time to block it. After four hours, the battle ended. The army of Jan Kazimir lost 30 thousand field soldiers, 29 thousand horse's soldiers, and 35 cannons. Such losses are half of the entire military. This is irretrievable defeat.

Kazimir ordered the surviving troops to retreat through Kremenets to Zbarazh. Sam think s that the forces of the Cossacks will not attack more. Did not know well enough and stayed in Mizoch.

On the morning of August 18, from the flanks, Bogun attacked the 60 thousandth army. From the front, the army of Necha, diverting blows to the rear, another fresh reserve Cossack regiment. King Jan Kazimir ran out of the chambers and in only his underwear runs away with a thousand guard.

Having run away so quickly, he compelled to wait four more hours for the remains of his army under the village of Mosty, which turned out to be only 15,000 people. Further retreating with the army near the town of Green Oak, another ambush divides the surviving, and a large half end up being surrounded by scintillating fire. Vishnivetsky with Jan Kazemir hid in Zbarozh.

November 26, 1651 - Ivan Bohun, Nechai, Morozenko, and Cirocco broke Yarema with his four hired garrisons, and the executioner and traitor Vishevetsky bashfully fled to Poland. He left the army in battle near Zborov alone. Polish King Jan Kazimir immediately asks to talk with Bohun about returning to Poland. Ivan Bohun lets him go with the condition and promise that he will never step on Ukrainian land again. Bohun defeating the newly created army of the Polish gentry with Jesuit roots and financing August 29, Ivan Bohun defeats them all with ease. After these events, King Jan Casimir abdicated and leaves to France to live in a monastery.

For some reason, the chronicles lose the chronology of these events. Moreover, all this is attributed to Khmelnitsky at that time no longer the militant hetman army of Zaporozhye. Like the nonexistent and never-seen Belotserkovsky treaties, as another falsification of history. This was a new device in history, which happened for the first time entirely by accident. When Jan Kazimir secretly sent the latter with a message to the Jesuits about victory, already on August the 3rd.

Later Ivan Bohun, doubly famous for his exploits, married a Ukrainian girl called Odarochka and they had two boys together.

After Vygovsky's victory in the fratricidal war and win over the Moscow army was defeated by those who were against both Poland and the Moscow Tsar, because of which weakened the military and killed hundreds of thousands of Cossack souls in battles among themselves. Were unable to fight and as a result, under the authority of the Moscow kingdom, which at its discretion each time changed the terms of the signed articles which were not shown to anyone. Then they say that they even lost it altogether until the Cossacks were banned and until the Sich was destroyed. For half a millennium Ukraine fell under the power and slavery of the Moscow regime. Chaos reigned in the era of decline and ruins in the history of Ukraine. From that moment on, the enemies tried to eradicate everything that was Ukraine and what it was in reality. That Ukrainians were their people, destroying Ukrainian history, changing facts, ruining the traditions of life, fame, word, soul, faith, truth.

Conspirators in the survey represent Zaborovskie documents clearly show their lack of connection with the time in which occurred the events described above.

In the middle of this slavish existence and attempts to destroy the Ukrainian true Russian nationality, race, land, faith, truth, taking everything from being rich earlier Ukraine, trying to spread its speech. Eradicate people by famine, Taras Grigorovich Shevchenko became a new beginning for Ukraine.

Taras Grigorovich Shevchenko only with the words along with some other great writers revived the language and forced people to remember and fight in words, and if it is necessary to compete with the new force for Ukraine. Now in free Ukraine: 90% of the population at least knows their history and language, 70% of them use Ukrainian every day, and 40% understandably speak only Ukrainian language, and this number is only growing.

They began to torment Ukraine and destroy it from all sides at the end of the seventeenth century.

The glorious Zaporozhye Cossacks with Colonels Ivan Bohun and Serk refused to swear allegiance to the Moscow Tsar to their tragic end in the war for an independent Ukraine. Bohun was in the west with Poland.

Moscow took a wait-and-see stance, trying in any negotiations get the signed articles by Khmelnytsky before his death. Which at that time, they were not under the power to show, and after a while, they were supposedly lost.

Mules for the order of the Sultan prayed for the death of the Kosh hetman Sirk.

Sirk had 55 battles and didn't lose a single one. For the Tatars and Turks, he was Urus-shaitan. Finally, irritated by the constant raids of the Cossacks, Mehmel the fourth sends a letter to Sich with an appeal to the Cossacks.

"I, the Sultan and the lord of the Sublime Porte, the son of Ibrahim. I, brother of the Sun and the Moon, the grandson. Viceroy of God on earth, the lord of the kingdoms of Macedon, Babylon, Jerusalem, Great and Lesser Egypt. The king over the kings, the ruler over the lords. The incomparable knight, warrior, ruler of the tree of life, an unshakable custodian of the grave of Jesus Christ, the trustee of God himself, the hope and consoler of Muslims, the intimidator and the great defender of Christians.

I command you, Zaporozhye Cossacks, to surrender voluntarily, and without any resistance and me with yours, attacks do not bother."

Sultan of Turkey Mehmed IV.

Answer from Zaporozhtsev Mohammed IV to the Turkish Sultan:

You, the Sultan, the devil of Turkey and the accursed devil brother and companion, Lucifer secretary. What the hell are you a knight when you can't kill a hedgehog with your naked ass? The devil you, your face is gone. You will not have Christian sons under your rule, you son of a bitch; we are not afraid of your army, we will fight with you with earth and water.

Babylonian you cook, Macedonian chariot, Jerusalem brewer, Alexandrian Kozolup, Big and Small Egypt swineherd, Armenian thief, Tatar Sagaidak, Kamenets executioner, all the world and the fictitious fool and our dick hook. You're a pig, a muzzle, a butcher's dog, an unbaptized forehead, and just for god's sake fuck your mother. Kozolup! (the one who rips goats' skins; also, in a figurative sense, one who has sexual relations with goats.)

That's how you answered the Zaporozhye, the shabby Sultan. You will not even hold the hogs of Christians.

We end with this, since we do not know the numbers, and we do not have a calendar, a month in the sky, a year in the book, a day, like your day, for all this kiss my ass!"

I have signed: Kosher ataman Ivan Sirko along with the whole camp Zaporozhye.

Kazakov remembered world history in opera, musical works, symphonies, sketches, novels, short stories, poems, poems, works of art. For example, only a small part which created masterpieces of the world's treasure - "Mazepianu" about Hetman Ivan Mazepa:

Francischak Gosetsky 1732, Henri Constant d'Orville, 1764, Henry Bertuha 1820, John Howard Payne. 1852.

Europe knew about Mazepa from the works of Voltaire, Pushkin, Releev, Victor Hugo and Byron, with the symphonic poem of Francis Liszt, the opera of Peter Ilyich Tchaikovsky, and the paintings of Vernet. The main one among all, among many relatives and dear Ukrainians, rightfully consider Ivan Petrovich Kotlyarevsky.

The world-famous art of the Cossack era was the canvas of Ilya Repin Reply of the Zaporozhian

Cossacks to Sultan Mehmed IV of the Ottoman Empire, also known as Cossacks of Saporog Are Drafting a Manifesto.

Unharness the horses, guys

And lie down to take a rest.

And I will go in the garden green,

To dig the little well there.

(Refrain.)

Mary one! Two! Three! Guelder rose, brunette girl,

Take the berries in the garden (twice)

I was digging the little well

In the green garden.

Maybe will come this girl

To take the water very early in the morning?

(Refrain.)

The girl has come

To make the water very early morning.

And a Cossack is following her

To bathe his horse.

He asked her the bucket -

She did not give it to him.

He gave a ring for her hand -

She did not take it.

I know, I know, my girl,

Why you are so upset.

Cause yesterday's evening

I was talking to another girl.

She is small and very young,

She has the blond braid to the waist

And there is the blue ribbon in her braid.

At the crossroads, the kobzar sits and plays on the harp. Guys sit around like the poppy is flourishing.

Kobzar plays, sings, pronounces words, how the Muscovites horde and Poles fought with the Cossacks.

They met all together on Sunday morning. How the Cossack was buried in a green ravine. Kobzar plays sing a song called - Even misfortune laughs

At the crossing, the kobzar is sitting

But playing on the Kobza;

Around guys and girls -

How poppy is flourishing?

Playing kobzar, singing

Pronunciation in words

Like Muscovites, hordes, straps

Fought with the Cossacks;

How was the ghost girl going?

On Sunday in the morning;

How to hide a Kozachenko

In the green rampage.

Playing kobzar, singing -

It's a bad laugh ...

There was once a time with hetman, and it will not come back.

There was a time we reigned, and it will not come back!

Those glory of the Cossack Eye will not be forgotten!

T.G. Shevchenko.

To some, it all can seem exciting and so it is, but this is not just a story. It's real life, and real life is full of suffering and sorrow. Along with the sacrifices of one's presence on the altar of the future for its people, for a life in which we all live now. We all forget what these generations of people survived and the fear of what was happened at the time. Especially the cruelties that were punishments for Cossacks when they were put at stake. Starting with the Cossack Mamai and ending with whole Cossack families in Ukraine all these centuries. All these centuries of slavery from the cruel neighbor's Muscovites and Poles, as well as millions of slaves stolen by the Tatars all on top of a thousand years of lies about our history.

I successfully passed history and all my other exams and got into a university that is one of the top three in the country. Of course, I left my parents. I didn't have more strength to be with them in the same house anymore. Parents often do not understand children. I thought it all over and told them that I loved them and that this was it. I put the phone down and immediately went to the club.

My soul was burning with flame, and my heart falls apart with thousands of fragments and nothing, nothing could help me, even books about history. The world classics, which were not just fascinating, it aroused hatred in me for the fact that our world is still so far from perfect and generally so unfair!

Someone will say "ah boy..." for all those who have loved know these sufferings, as well as this love which can unite the present that was in life. And once you lose this peace, you can no longer find it.

As you get age, you can't help but love with a pure heart. Everything that happens now is just a sequence of events in which I must find meaning. I promise not to betray myself anymore and find myself in the fact that I will do anything for anyone. For myself, I no longer deserved anything, I put myself in slavery to all simple people, like the Cossacks.

In the name of love, I betrayed, not keeping anyone else's hope for anything. I couldn't awake my heart. I know it did not hear me, and the universe let a new path show and let it be whatever it will be.

Now I'm a servant with the world on his shoulders, a selfish animal, despise those who are not right and all the evil that exists. The most important thing is that everything I know it's all during this lifetime.

Young people often do not understand it all, do not understand the extent of their knowledge. They are always trying to prove their truth in a variety of issues. Seeing this, I laugh in their face, such hypocrites, such swine that can't be cleaned, change everything in yourself and find oneself and all this I will do to help myself now. It makes no sense to live as before, something new is in front, but still so far away, and can't reach the moment when I can say:

"Stop! From this moment on, everything will always be different!"

I'm still such a young fool. The only thing that can soothe me is a bottle of wine, another one with the light turned off in an empty apartment where now I live myself with this beautiful view of the night Kiev. I am here with silence and with this view of the motherland. Both banks of the Dnieper are seen with a cigarette lug on the window sill of another dull summery day, for those who walk on the ground below the sixth floor.

"Frost, the metro, finally we'll soon get home. It just we gotta go through the whole student campus..."

In the bustle of the city at night, quickly, glancing at the door from the platform, noticed the starry sky. In a not so large crowd that usually tears to the escalator at the station, my best friend, Volodya, who was studying with me at university and was an enterprising man in his nature, heard me, but did not say anything in reply:

"In my opinion, it is so beautiful and wonderful."

"And what's this? For the summer holidays, you can go to the USA as students?" I read on the Signboard

"Yes, my friend has already gone twice; it's very cool," replied Volodya, finally.

"I would love to go!"

"Yeah? Do you even know any English?"

"I don't care."

"America is a great country. I always wanted to go, but I'm probably not as brave as you, to take up and go by myself. You can at any time, catch your luck and go, and everything will come out . Maybe you'll seduce a girl or woman there and will stay. I would do that, but I have plans and my future career here. Well, I told you, I did not go when there was an opportunity for me. Now I'm regretting it. I wish that everything would work out for you! So as a friend, I tell you to go!

Without a doubt!" said Volodya confidently.

Of course, father with some convincing, but gave out money, because this is good practice. Once when they were young, they did not get a visa to the United States. I'm sure my father would have been very successful there. Bureaucracy, courts, corrupt state apparatus kills regular business in our country. The profits of such a level specialist abroad were dozens of times more than in the same companies here in Ukraine.

So, at the end of spring, I packed my backpack, and full of enthusiasm was ready to fly to the famous place where it is so beautiful, fashionable, where not everyone could go. I was like DiCaprio who rushes on the Titanic in a thirst for new adventures and discoveries on the way to America.

Volodya is my perfect friend and since the most important thing for us at home is to know the right people. Volodya had this all. The main thing is that ties are everywhere. I always had friends with connections. For example, Volodya could solve anything without any problems, even closing the university session for a couple of months before. So, while everyone was just about to prepare for the exams, I was already going to the airport with good grades for the end of the year and state scholarship, trust me this possibility for knowledgeable people. It is essential.

The United States! The homeland of surprising celebrities, legends and those who came there and gained fame.

Just look at those cities: New York, Los Angeles, Chicago and Miami, exactly where I was heading. It was impossible not to think "please, can I at least get there!" sitting in the tail of the aircraft and being afraid in the heart. My knees tremble with the understanding that this hefty aluminum thing will be able to fly such distances at such a height and with such speed. The wings will not break off somewhere above the Atlantic. No, it's the same thing as Titanic, but only in the air. I now understand and enjoy. Even as you already guessed, I'm afraid to fly. I'm sitting, and behind me are just tanks with fuel, because I'm at the very tail. Well, take-off, a dreadful din, I squeezed into the seat of the roller coaster, and I sit, getting more and more vertical, so high up!

Conclusion: Do not take a seat in the tail. A thought flashed, what a pity that life is finite. That only once we can experience something for the first time and that when there is no love, whatever we try, and whatever we feel, we can't get used to it.

Irochka is my favorite wherever she is now and whether she thinks of me. We flew out of the clouds, the flight straightened. I could not tear myself away from the view through the porthole. May God ever have mercy and forgive me, and fate will forgive me and give me another chance. Maybe I'm closer to God now, and if you can hear me now because I'm closer to you than people on earth. Then I want to say that you must have mercy on us and help us all on this earth!

I calmed down and after a few deep sighs looked in the salon and became just one of those who are there. Only those who are flying somewhere. Only one of those who now live on earth. The enumeration number in the table of life is a unit or even zero.

After nine hours, I flew to New York JFK Airport, where I slept in uncomfortable chairs, waiting for a transfer. Another five in Atlantic City, where I had to get to the suburbs of Miami, where I had a job contract.

When I got out of the airport, I was shocked. I knew that Americans liked big cars, but to be like that!?

I was amazed, and the hot summer sun of Florida shone in a particularly beautiful way. It already came out of the zenith and even approached it to start an editing decline to a ghost. Which would happen to me for the rest of my life.

A few minutes later I found a restaurant with delicious burgers and I was about to take my backpack and leave when a passing girl bumped into me:

"Oh, I am sorry."

"Don't worry. It's alright. Are you ok?"

"Oh, are you Russian?" she asked in Russian with a slightly noticeable accent. She is brightly smiling with a sparkling with her eyes.

"Aah Yes and You?" I replied in Russian.

Her appearance was quite stunning: short shorts, brown boots, crop-top. But I did not show my surprise. I already knew during the year of active nightlife in Kiev how to communicate with girls.

Although my soul was sad and probably it could be seen in my eyes. Even when I was in a good mood, and this was like many girls. Although at this moment, like either after meeting with Ira or when I was a child. My eyes were bright and joyfully burned, and I was 100 percent frank. I hate hypocrisy, I want to and will remain myself. But passing by the person, I will also smile like here in America. That's what I like best about here. Oh! This world is entirely different. America is great. Those who have not seen the United States cannot and do not have the right to judge the country.

"You're strange, eloquent, cool … well, also handsome." said this girl in the brown boots.

I swear that's what she said and it surprised me. This style is much steeper than those proud faces which then willingly, as dolls for the dressed-up young cute boy, would give a blowjob or fuck in the toilet.

Yes, I've become like that, for now, while I'm in grief and it's been for a long while, but I'll change.

"I was born here, but my parents are from Russia, they are divorced. I'm old enough to live on my own. Where are you going?"

"Well, actually, I just left the plane and am headed for the suburb in Miami."

"Oh, and I'm in Miami, to see my mother. Have you already bought a metro ticket?"

"Not yet, I was just about to."

"I have a Honda, stuffed with things, but I think your backpack will fit in."

"Aren't you afraid to go with a strange guy? You're such a sweet girl, and all that..."

"No, you seem to be a very decent guy and very handsome. If I had to pick someone at the first look, I would have stopped at you. I propose to pretend to be a very nice couple. The door does not work to get in through the open window. You are not going behind the wheel."

"It's scorching here, but it does not prevent us from going to watch the sunset and enjoy it. Just the two of us. Just like young lovers and blah blah."

"Oh, yes my husband is a romantic. How lucky I am! That will happen when you get to Miami. It is very high humidity."

"I don't know about the humidity, but I know that I'm shocked by this world. It's like another reality!

Can I drive?"

"It depends on whether you know how to drive. Also, whether you have a DL. I think that since you just arrived. When the first three months they must work, so go ahead if you want."

"And you know, you look wonderful in this chair. I, of course, are very pleased with your compliments, but often the first look is deceptive. You do not know me at all."

"Let's not talk about this. Forget about everything and drive."

"It is just amazing! I cannot believe that I'm driving along the road going to Miami. I am fortunate. I have not felt so great for a long time. I am very pleased to have met you."

"Do not be so sweet."

I have a beautiful CD with the music of old legends, as I call them. Thus the first four hours of driving on the highway were the most joyful in the last six months of my life. As well as the most interesting. We talked about unfulfilled desires and about what happened in our lives and how we want to realize ourselves. I shared with her everything I thought about, that tormented my soul.

We just laid into each other with the stories of our lives. With genuine expressions, exchanging the experience, joy, and sorrow. We even stopped once to hug. We laughed and talked about our dreams.

"Why don't we stop at this hotel. it's too late or are you going to go into the night?"

I immediately turned back. We went in and booked a room.

"Can you sleep with a stranger?"

"Well, first of all, you are my husband. Secondly, do not try to spoil this novel."

The hotel, like everything else, was a simple and at the same time such an unusual place. We went into our room and she neatly started taking off my shirt.

We laughed and kissed. The first words that were pronounced instantly "In the Shower?"

"Do not touch the switcher, darling. Enjoy the silence, love, with all your heart, as if this is your love, your Ira..."

I turned around. Her red eyes from crying, we wrapped each other in a big hug. I lay with my back on the bed, and her body wriggled over me. We changed in the erotic fire of our desires, we were one whole, and our passion was irreversibly free. Secure with the fullness of feelings in our hearts, full of love, which at that time lived in us. We felt it with our whole body, and only we knew then. Why...?

We stopped at different places along the way. Threw French fries in the car, listened to music, kissed and smiled at each other. We ate ice cream that melted under the hot rays of the sun and incredible stuffiness, such as high humidity. Looking up at the clear sky, it seemed that the sun would burn you alive, we wished we could stay on that road forever!

In the next hotel a few kilometers near my place, I woke the morning to see beside me on the pillow a little note:

"I wish you happiness and love, and no matter how much I want to stay with you forever. I do not want you ever to suffer being with me. I'm not who you need. I'm married; I'm sorry I did not say. Yes, there are women like this. I do not like it, but because of the money, I'll be with him. You're the best I've ever had. Goodbye.

P.S. Why did I do it with you? I am not sure, but I know you will still meet your love. I would like you not to lose yourself, because there are no many men like you, unfortunately."

"Not to lose yourself," I said in a voice reading the note, "Another sin, well, thank you. just what I wanted!"

I was placed in a house with some students like me. In neighboring houses, which are all rented on the coast, there were American students. Those who decided to spend their entire lives at the resort. The view from the window could not fail to impress my eyes and mind. For the first time in front of me, there was so much water and the realization that some force in front of me is. How all the same it is incredible and unusual. White sand, which nowhere else in the world, can be found.

Two-dollar delicious pizza, when you earn $ 8 per hour and get the best whiskey in the world for $25 and how to smoke with a neighbor the best quality Cuban cigars. Richard, and his girlfriend Terry and his slobbering dog Gracie. They were just beautiful, but it was clear to see with them drinking alcohol from morning to night; their skin was already decaying well. They were around 55 years old.

They were living together already long time after they left the families that were with them before. All Americans are just like these; my neighbors are amiable. Looking at them, I felt sorry for them people in Europe.

It turns out that we are all the same, all with our own tragic stories from which the listener gets tears in their eyes. And everyone, each has his tragedy in this world. We all live in the world that owns us, our lives. At such times, you want to scream that everything is wrong and it's time to change everything, and want to shout it all over the world. People decide that in this life for other people when everyone should have an equal right to vote in any matter. Then according to what rules we live now, we are prone to. This is ordinary logic, an average person who has at least slightly climbed out of his society, its reality. Here in America, it's the same as in their film. This is their world.

Take even the house of my parents: the fireplace, the high wooden floor, the walls made of stone.

All in a grand style, somehow. Take our streets and their streets. Frankly, I'm surprised that it's all there, it seems like a sort of fairy tale and somehow an incredible reality. Honestly, I would live in this reality.

I would like so that all people could live like this. How can it be that just a few miles from the border?

People live according to stupid laws where the car is two to three times more expensive. Where there are no regular salaries and so on? Yes, this is the material world, but here anyone can start to work honestly and become a respected person. Our people there went through such horror, and so many troubles that not a single word can describe it and people there still live in such injustice. Maybe my destiny is to try to do something.

Although if I go into politics, anything could happen even murder. On the other hand, without casualties, it is impossible to win, or as they say:

"If you are afraid of wolves, don't go into the forest."

All this I was saying, quite drunk to Richard and Teri who catered the joy in me. Which was the first time for me, I tried to explain that in my broken English. They listened attentively to me, trying to grasp the meaning. As it turned out, I managed to explain everything correctly using my meager, as a man studying English since childhood. It was especially funny when I said these two phrases about the forest and the wolf at the end. I explained everything to them, and we talked about life for a long time.

From the height of their years. They wished me luck in trying, trying to do something and achieve it in this life. They already understood that everything was over for them. It was written on their faces. Of course, I did not share my thoughts. We said good-bye and always, then when we saw each other on the street or when we went out onto the balcony. We chatted and laughed a lot.

The same evening, I somehow managed to see something that had been in front of me before, then when I smoked that joint, I went to sleep immediately, it cut me off altogether. On that first wonderful evening, people were walking along the night beach with lights. We're catching crabs, burning the fires on the beach right in front of our house where there were about three hundred apartments wherein the first line. Above us, the beautiful sky of the Gulf of Mexico was beautiful.

I cannot believe that there are people who live their whole lives in their villages.

If all people went to live in America at least for three months and returned, then a lot would change. But not just go and see, really live there.

Our state system would have seemed to them delirium in the appearance and the problem it's all in the order, and not in people.

Before the road, I decided to rest for a couple of days and left the house for a walk. One girl came to meet me. I recognized her; I met her even when I just came and saw her since then often. She worked on the spot near my house in one of the surfboard shops.

She also decided to take a walk. We walked along the beach, full of silence, under the dark sky and dark, not because the sun had already set. It was only 4 pm but because the clouds covered all the sky and the air seemed so close that you could reach and even touch these vast clouds. In this place, the world is flattened, where the ocean and the clouds go into each other as if this is the end of the world.

We stand in front of all this enormous power and cannot move from what we see like everything else among the stillness of the ocean. The warm air that gusts us with such force that it gives goose bumps. While there are flashes of lightning among these dark clouds, though still far away, and the sea is still insanely calm, but terrifyingly looks directly into our soul. It seemed that you couldn't find a scarier place, or more beautiful.

She behaved herself, so nothing was happening around, as always, she was animatingly telling something, waving her hands and laughing. We sat down on one of the numerous bridges that are located on the spit.

"Hug me," she said softly, "Why you didn't come to visit me for all this time? Didn't I call you many times? I do not understand how, the boy, who I liked all summer, met again each other only now? When we met accidentally a long time ago?" She continued.

I did not have time to answer as she kissed me.

"I do not know what to say to you, except that my heart was not ready yet, as it is not ready now."

"Yes, I see it in your eyes. Although I have never experienced this, looking at you, I understand how important it is to you," She added and put her hand on my heart.

We said goodbye before it got too dark and went home.

Four hours later, my plane left.

I went to Washington with friends after Atlanta. We walked around almost everywhere in one day after we drove on a smelly and freezing bus to New York. It was terrible, but when I saw New York. It was straight, WOW!

Of course, I was impressed with the statue of Liberty and skyscrapers and even Brooklyn, in which we lived for four days. And then I got on an airplane and flew to my homeland, my native home. It was a beautiful summer. I realized that I'm sort of alive and should start all over again. But Ukraine in my eyes was already so gray and quite different than America. America is a country of possibilities or merely a choice of life. A life where everyone, doing regular work, can afford a simple average life. The car, the house all this is available here to ordinary people, and quickly.

You can live allowing yourself everything if you are ready to work, if you want more and feel that you can draw in university. Please go and learn, and if you want that, spiritual development can always be found.

Honestly, I felt and understood that neither spiritually nor morally, I was not yet selenium. Thinking about all this, I watched the news, and it turned out that I had barely time to leave Florida. On August 19, 2008, there was a big tropical storm "Fei" that took a cyclone, which took thirty-four thousand lives. Of course, I didn't know if my friends, my acquaintances, who become dear people to me, are still alive.

My return was joyful and full of impressions. Of course, I was glad to return home on the other side; I was broken inside. When I got back, I realized that only I had changed. That everybody and everything had remained the same, and that immediately started to hamper me. Since I worked all summer long and I forgot what a dream is. Immediately started study back in university, that in my understanding became not interesting to me. My father even took from me all the money that I earned. I did not also buy myself an iPhone. All since I promised him this money back, that he invested. I agreed, this is a business, albeit insulting. Of course, he still gave me money and paid for everything, so I did not care. By the new year, I even bought a new iPhone, but in my studies, which was nothing unusual for me anymore. in the measure of my lack of general knowledge, I stopped being an excellent student and a candidate for a red diploma . I cringed and almost got kicked out of the university on the winter semester. Although I was sure that I wrote everything as it should be. I had to connect the connections, to ask influential people to help resolve the issue.

I liked everything at home, but the money for which I was offered to work parallel with study in the companies. To put it mildly, was ridiculous, and my parents said to enjoy the student life and pull at least in university.

Of course, the misconduct with all the teachers about almost being kicked out was catching up to me now. Something else happened in this time. When I arrived, I told some friends that I had tried the weed for the first time. It turned out that in Ukraine, many smokers do more also sniff and pick up girls on this subject. Of course, I immediately began to look at all of them severely, and after half a year, also began to smoke regularly.

"You know, guys, the grass here is completely different, it also smells so strange...", I Said.

"Well, it's not America. Let's go outside?" Said one of my friends.

"Well, let's have one more. We'll go to the night session; we'll take the girls and champagne. It will be great," Said another one of my friends.

This way, I lived in a new pace, prolonged but enjoyable from the constant traffic of life. I thought at that moment that it all looked like a black canvas in the center of New York. These were the streets that I suddenly looked from the other side. Those streets that in New York in the present had become obsolete different. It seemed that we just caught up with the time that right now can only be seen in the old films. I always on a subconscious level, analyzed what was happening around me.

The grayness of the houses and the sad frowning faces of passing by people, with angry on whole world eyes, bother me so much. In the awareness of all this, this life, I tried not to dive into the thoughts that were hammering my head. The reality for them is life as it's, and unreality it's an experience where a person deserves to live, making a dream come true.

Once again, stoned, I just sat in the room, thinking that this can't go on, and I do not need to be stoned to understand this. Usually, you feel good or bad, and this is just bad.

Suddenly, someone knocked on the door. I opened.

"Hello, Willy, I have a great weed, let's go! Oh, I see you already," asked my friend.

"Yes, come on, buddy, smoke it yourself. Then we'll go out into the street. I'll smoke a cigarette, while everything will blow. I'll tell you something. By the way, this is the last time in my life I smoke weed", I answered.

"You know, today it's just another ordinary day!" Said I.

"I would not say it's clear weather. I cannot smoke cigarettes. I'd rather smoke weed, " said, and threw a cigarette on the asphalt.

"Here's the trash can," I picked up a cigarette and threw it in the garbage.

"All that you just said is complete nonsense because you've already got the brains out of the grass.

For all three years that you're smoking," He continued.

"Yet it has been proven that it kills human brain cells. This is an uncontested fact, and that says it all, "said I am protecting myself.

Suddenly a woman passing by, half-turned on us, said, "Jesus loves you."

"Yes, I understand everything, but your words are not enough for me," He said.

"Firstly, you contradict yourself all the time. So I will not even listen to you. The second you heard what this woman said? She said, 'Jesus loves you.' Did you hear that?" I asked.

"Yes. What is it? She just was weird," He answered.

"Well, then, as I said, it's especially. That says it all!!!" I repeat.

I came home and realized that I was wasting my time. I'd better help those who understand this and want to change their lives. And why am I going to do this? Yes, because I will do it for myself, to save my life. I can do it so that at least someone else could also change their lives. For half a year, I did not see my parents again. Summer was coming. So I decided to earn money to give my parents money back.

Many of my friends left after graduating from university, moved to their apartments, and got a job. So when I had a day off. I often went to the club myself in the middle of the week. There was always a lot of people. It's summer, and it was blackout nights, often not even remembering how I got home or at all.

I would wake up in someone else's apartment with one of the girls that I met at the club. It was normal; it was my new life. You stand behind the bar, drinking glass after glass.

You meet with a glance fleetingly. You immediately understand what they want from you, because she already waits for this look half a night. You do not even need to say anything and also get acquainted. You just come up and take what you need, or she will even approach herself, asking for a cigarette. Although she may not even smoke, and the fate of the night is already sealed. The main thing is not to spoil her fantasy. All that needs to be done is take her appearance. If you have it, do not talk too much so she would not be interested in talking to you. Doing all that, you have ninety-nine percent success when meeting with a glance. You do not need a name, and often I did not even hear it, covering her sweet lips with: "We don't need words" - half drunk and ready for everything now, in the current moment. Which is the most important and which is so fabulous, full of pathos, martini, music and whiskey world.

One year later, my life has become swift and exciting. This whole year I, am intensely engaged, and I must say I have achieved for myself the significant successes. Once you pass these last exams, you realize how your life depends on it, even worse, how your actions and deeds can influence other people.

Especially if it's all about your relatives, whom you love most and then disappoint them with each step. When already something that does not change at all. Although new moments come that you can rejoice, already with a calm soul. It seems like a time try to forget and leave everything in the past, the past its unneeded cargo. The past must be remembered. The past must be overcome in oneself, to find the future. Of course, I did not pass the exams correctly, but I already knew exactly what I should do.

I went to a therapist who had already stopped teaching. My classmate helped me and arranged for a couple of sessions. Knowingly in the US, even children sometimes go to a psychiatrist. Now, I knew it for sure. It was enough that I start to remember why did it all begin. In childhood, me and my Dad liked to play table tennis and somehow one day me, my dad and my grandfather were somewhere together. Grandfather called me to go for a couple of days to stay with him, and my father asked if I want to visit him. Maybe we'll go home and play table tennis. I said that I would go to my grandfathers. In the eyes of my father, then, I saw the agreement with a bitter taste of resentment and disagreement in my choice. But not for me, because I did not pay much attention to this. My father , after that, no longer played with me in tennis and even folded the table for many years, and I just started to win from him. I beat all my friends at the expense of it. This is the only thing he taught me, although no, first I learned to play in the camp. Then, to attract his attention, I began to steal and did not understand what was happening. Even asked God to help me to stop, but this is psychology, human psychology. I can't blame my Dad for it - this is also nature. Whose fault is it? A system in which the Father cannot recognize such a simple error and rightly correct the situation, do not start the sequence of mistakes. Which happens in the relations of parents and children.

Since ten years old, I blamed him for not paying attention to me at all, and he told me that I was a bad son. That I was disappointing him. I always tried to change from that moment, and become even more confused by misunderstanding. There were such moments when he called me bad words, and I dreamed of never seeing him again.

Of course, from the first heartbeat up to now, the sensible explanation was not found, and doctors didn't have anything to offer except pills, time and getting it all out, which didn't help.

Further education and life, I chose a program for students in London. I was finishing the 4th course.

Speaking frankly about everything that happened to me in Ukraine since childhood, the whole system of the government. Even my parents, who were more comfortable to love in the distance pushed me only in one direction, to leave and never come back again.

Before retiring, I decided to endure the fast.

"I hope you understand what kind of work it is? And that you do not just have to pray, you also must fast." Asked my Mom.

"Mom just say, what exactly you need to do." Said I.

My Mom, Dad, the family I love you so much. God, please forgive me and help me.

I tried to feel through the prayers that I read. I decided to understand what was happening to me and how I should continue. These a few months have become very important for me. As if I was, just at the time where I supposed to be and then waking up in the morning. I just remembered my childhood and how great it was to wake up knowing that my family was close and that they loved me. I felt careless and happiness that I wanted to sit at the table and write poetry. I remembered how I once wanted to write a book. I began to form an idea. The hope that I've been looking for so long has caught fire in my eyes. For me, it's just a book, and a book about the past seems to be describing essential things for my life. But I do not even suspect what's going to happen in the future and what fate has in store.

What the words are with the rot that flooded our society into the sea of which drowns every day with the hope of salvation.

Having got to confess not to that priest, that I wanted I was not much disappointment but expressed everything. It seems to me from the stories about my adventures and life that this young priest was carried away, and the notes of human vices skipped instead in the apparent discussion of my life. I did not like kneel. In the Bible, it is written that one can stand only before God on his knees.

Mom always loved me and supported me. We walked with her around the city in which I was born.

Where she happily grew up with her parents in early childhood. She offered to buy a chair with a different back for the spine, but I said that it is not necessary that I already will buy it in Canada. She also asked not to burn all the bridges before leaving. As she was feeling my mood to go forever and not return.

We had a great time then, and in the evening. I went up to my father and asked for forgiveness for everything, in return, I heard a mean, "Okay!"

"You do not want to tell me anything?" I objected.

He did not say anything. I did not mention either. It was clear, after that «Okay» that this man doesn't want to understand something in this life.

Although this is just probably his type of character. Thinking it all, I went to my room. It made me so amused, this situation, that I even started to laugh. Of course, my father was already far away and did not hear that I was laughing. Otherwise, it would undoubtedly be disrespectful. I thought about this, after all, how many people are so stubborn, who have their truth. Their vision or which by their nature cannot change themselves. How then can I change the mindset of all that needs to be changed and set up for all one life in which we all must move in one direction? It's funny. The conclusion is one and obvious only systematically!

I love my parents; they are such kind souls and always will be dear to my heart. My sister is the best person on earth.

One day I went down the stairs and heard that my mother was crying in the living room. I remember I been 13 years already. She was lying on the bed, facing the wall. On the outside was a bright sunny day.

I quietly entered the room; she turned around. I neatly lay down next to her and looked into her beautiful, full of depths and sadness light blue tear-stained eyes:

"Mom, what happened. Why are you crying?"

"Nothing. I remembered something. Where are you going?"

"At the stadium with the guys. We are at the Lyceum agreed today on training."

"Are you smoking? I found a pack of cigarettes in your jacket".

"No, it's not mine, it's Kira, she just left it at mine. I'm doing sports; I can't. What did you try to find in my jacket?"

"Well, you, as always, threw it and did not hang it. You know that my dad also smoked. He died when I was eleven. William, don't smoke, please, okay?"

Her alarmed voice always touched me to the depths of my soul.

"Okay Mammy, I will not. I will not, but I do not need these checks. I said that I'm doing everything right and I know how to act."

"You have such a character, try to get along more with people. You have a beautiful heart. You are smart, but your incontinence and struggle for independence hinder your progress. Do not rush, learn more, while we are here, you will have time to live an adult life. My dad could never get on in the team. He suffered from this, although he had great posts, he could not stay long. Because if only someone says something to him, he could not stand the instructions and criticism. He left, he could flare up, drink, smoke and come home, like you this Saturday. Dad said that he heard you come in the door, drunk, and then talked on the phone for two hours and fighting with somebody. I'm so afraid for you, and I do not want you to be like my father. My mom suffered from this. That's why she died so early too. This vodka, I wish it'll all be burned up, can spoil your whole life with its muck. Do not succumb to this; be stronger and smarter."

"Okay, mammy, it's all good, we celebrated victory, but I promise that I will work on it. Mammy, everything will be fine. I love you very much. I'm in a rush, but, please, do not worry. Everything will be fine, you'll see."

A month later, my little sister, sitting in my room, said to me: "Willie, our mother got sick. She was put in the hospital, so you get on with it and hold on, support Daddy. But do not say anything, as if you do not know anything."

One evening, my father returned late from work, I turned off the light and saw through the window how he somehow got out of the car uncertainly. He went into the house and immediately fell asleep.

In the morning we picked up sister and mom, all the way in the car, everyone was silent. The next day at home, I found out that my mother was sick with cancer. Her illness was entirely neglected and needed a lot of money. But I still did not understand everything, although it all, I was amazed.

I did not know how to perceive it. Mom left again. A woman started cooking for me and my Dad, one mom hired, but we did not like the way she cooked. I even went to the market in the car that my father gave me. It was the same car, his first car, it was a red "six," and he hardly ever went to

the house. Only visited, and very rarely said something, we only sometimes met with glances. His eyes were red with fatigue. But still, he got up every morning before sunrise when I was still deeply asleep, and went to work. My mother came home from time to time, every time I noticed new changes. There was less hair on her head. I did not know how to talk to her. Time passed, and the fourth time she left, she smiled at me and said that this was the last trip, and everything would be fine. I hugged her and kissed her.

"Mammy, I love you very much, and I'm waiting."

"Everything is in the hands of the Lord," she answered. And she kept her word, coming back and staying with me, dad and sister. Six months later, my mother starts getting her hair back. She began to smile even more.

She watered her favorite lilies in the garden.

"Mammy, how are you?"

"Doctors said that I still need to drink vitamins, calcium, and everything else. And buy glasses, I became a little worse with the impaired vision."

I came closer, took her by the hand, and sat down next to her.

"Mammy, forgive me for everything that I do wrong. I will live so that I'll not upset you so that you will not be nervous.

"You know, I think it's a miracle, that I'm still with you, praying a lot and reading the Bible at the church in hospital. Even though I had a challenging stage and the doctors said that they could not promise anything. My life continued, I continued to believe as much as I could still think.

After a while, she would recover, but keep repeating: "... and thank God that He was with us and helped me, us. Dad, who worked so hard to earn money and gave him so much strength and patience. Today\ is a beautiful Sunday, and I go to church, do you want to join me?"

It's been such a long time, but not a day goes by that Mom does not thank for the miracle that happened to her and for every day she lives. Her faith is so strong!

I can no longer make mistakes. It's time to keep my word. I finally understand that our life is in our hands. I must honor and believe. If that's not enough, then I will do everything that I can.

How many people need to experience grief and suffering to understand what to believe in and how to live. How much more and how everything is? (My thoughts at the time). She cried so much in prayers for me, "God helps us all."

The destruction on April 26, 1986, of the fourth power unit of the Chernobyl nuclear power plant located on the territory of the Ukrainian SSR.

The Chernobyl nuclear power plant (51 ° 23'22 "N 30 ° 05'59" E) is located on the territory of Ukraine 3 km from the city of Pripyat, 18 km from the town of Chernobyl, 16 km from the border with Belarus and 110 km from Kiev.

Unlike the bombing of Hiroshima and Nagasaki, the explosion resembled a mighty "dirty bomb." The main damaging factor was radioactive contamination.

The first report on the Chernobyl accident appeared in the Soviet media on April 27, 36 hours after the explosion at the fourth reactor. The announcer of the Pripyat radio broadcasting network reported on the collection and temporary evacuation of the city residents.

April 28, 1986, at 21:00 TASS transmits a brief information message: "There was an accident at the Chernobyl nuclear power plant. One of the atomic reactors is damaged. Measures are being taken to eliminate the consequences of the crash".

The untimely, incomplete, and contradictory nature of official information about the catastrophe gave rise to many independent interpretations. Sometimes the victims of the tragedy are not only the citizens who died immediately after the accident but also residents of the adjacent areas who went to the demonstration for May 1st without knowing about the accident. With this calculation, the Chernobyl disaster significantly exceeds the atomic bombardment of Hiroshima by the number of casualties.

International organization Doctors Against Nuclear War argue that because of the accident only tens of thousands of people died from liquidators, in Europe 10,000 cases of congenital pathologies in newborns. Ten thousand cases of thyroid cancer and another 50,000 are expected.

According to the organization "Chernobyl Union," with 600,000 liquidators, 10% died and 165 000 became invalids.

Count the number of people with cancer in the territories that are most susceptible to infection, after the accident and to our time is impossible, but even having taken away the common statistical illness of people in the average statistical spot on the ground. As a result, of course, human activity on the planet earth, it is evident that even rough estimates of the experts shock your mind.

Almost every woman 95% can tell that in the days of the most radiation, they walked with children or participated in the parade under the unusually hot sun of the holiday of working people in the USSR. Without suspecting what was happening. This is not all an example of the fact that the Soviet Union is evil; it is that power and any concealment of the truth by the power of any country are set against people. My mother, that day was the same on a walk with my older sister, whom she was carrying in a stroller. Any information cannot be classified, and everything that happens in the world should be immediately publicized. Every situation should eventually be evaluated and decided in the shortest possible time because of a thorough study, because of which an absolute truth from which follows take visible instructions for the correct solution of the situation. Every case of any incident is a cancerous tumor in the body of the system of a nationwide organism.

Now in the world, there are 435 nuclear reactors, each of which can infect the whole planet with such an explosion.

I got a visa and go to England! One of the best place in the world! Real football and many think , but it's a different story. Of course, I meet new girls and, not a perfect, but I understood that at home it's home. Home it's best to place in the world for anybody in this world. We all should live in a place where we born and have the same life level of life in any position on the word. I still can understand why we have not one way for all countries. It's so easy to understand for ordinary people and so hard for people who not on the truth side!

After three years of traveling, I have been at home! What could be better than home, my mother, my father sister Shea with husband Bob, who become an older brother to nephews. Thank God I'm back, and now I'm here, closer. Mammy's borsch, a real Ukrainian one with vareniki with cherries. The native land, the sky, the air, people, how much you can appreciate, unlike those who have been here for a long time. Although our people are so friendly throughout all our Ukraine. In Donetsk, in Kiev, in Lviv, in Odessa, and throughout the Crimea, that the soul is in joy for them, as in such an impoverished country all of us, remain ourselves. All who live in our country in peace and happiness, it is probably a better land and history, but this is the country where I was born. This is the dream of which we all dreamed so much, how foolish I was that I wanted to go. Ukraine, as a girl we dream about and want it to be so accurate and correct to itself when the current girls are much different. We can see that this world is not going in the right way. I'm sure if they would follow their principles that a woman should live nearby. Then the guy will be what he needs to be, it is not just youth and not even youth adults, but at school for the school kids, where are the heads. Like the earth is all over with unformed personality and the nature of the interconnection of different parts of the brain and a dull look at life.

At home, when everyone else is asleep, I cannot fall asleep and meeting the sunrise standing in front of an open window on the second floor in the hall, wrapped in a blanket, with a cup of water natural and clear from the well. The smell of summer and the song of the nightingale in the garden are clearing my mind and my soul with the waves of pure love of the family home.

In a couple of days in the city again: Khreshchatyk, Bessarabka, Pechersk, Shulyavka and all our the native left bank of the Dnieper. The Dnieper the island on it, and the heavenly eyes of St. Sophia, the Postal and Kiev Pechersk Lavra, but the Moscow Patriarchate, and not the Ukrainian UOC.If that's the way it will be, then there will be no peaceful life and how it is so, when our church is the center of Russe and Christianity in Russe. Here should be the center.

A connection factor, both for Hitler's supporters and the USSR, was war.

If in the story of the salvation of the brotherly people of Hitler was Austria, then the Communists had Ukraine, with the myth of Bendery and friendly people. As the most famous person at that time who fought for the independence of Ukraine, when the Communists for the first-time seized Ukraine and made it a Soviet republic. About how the Red Army killed those who were wearing vishivanka (embroideries) when they visited Kiev and when they robbed and then, during the oppression of the Ukrainian people at 32-33-34 made artificial famines and sweeps of those who were against them and for the faith of Christ.

Events take us back to a time when they were whispering about Ukraine.

There is a reason that in Russia right now such a church "for people and truth, as well as power."

Father was a priest. Five-year-old child of the First World War. 1914 -1917, the village where Stepan grew four times experienced the invasions of the Austrians and the Imperial Army and the revolution in the ranks of the tsarist army of 1917. Since the time he witnessed the creation of the Western Ukrainian People's Republic and the proclamation of the act of sobornost. Already in 1918, the bloody War of Ukraine and Poland began, which ended in the complete seizure of the Galechina Poland. Blood, violence, and endless war, just like almost all the childhood of Stepan Bender passed. Stepan Bender was an ordinary student, he played and sang in the chorus, was a member of the theatrical circle.

Berlin McLenbugesh Strasse 73. Today no one paying attention to the strange, as for the Germans ornament on the front side under the roof of the house. (Ukrainian trident is more than 100 years old.) It was here that the UN headquarters in Germany. It was here that the first contacts of the Ukrainian nationalists with the German development were recorded. There was also the legendary Colonel Yevgeny Konovalets, the founder and permanent commandant of the Ukrainian People's Organization. It is known that at this time he lived in Germany and was looking for any support for the Ukrainian struggle for independence in the territory occupied by Poland. The Germans were interested in such cooperation and pursued an entirely different goal. The conquest of the eastern space.

The first for the invaders, but not for us Ukrainian in the beard for justice and its own independent country Ukraine. Shares of the company's propagandists were organized by Stepan Bender in the ranks of UON for the revival of the graves of Sich Riflemen, symbolizing the struggle for Ukrainian independence.

Anti-alcohol company.

UON called on all the conscious Ukrainians to stop smoking and not to drink alcohol, so as not to support the Polish monopoly on these goods, by the way. He never drank or smoked, and this for him has always been a principled position.

But the most significant action was school when children with the blue-and-yellow flags came out on the streets against the progressive reduction of schools in Galicia scandalized. We demand Ukrainian schools. It is this company that has gained wide publicity far abroad. Passed Roswit school, Amber, when Germany was not yet a Fascist Germany. The Germans bet on the organization, which led Bender. He was arrested from 1933 until June 15, 1939, when detachments of Ukrainian nationalists collaborated with German fascists to attack Poland and freed Bender from prison — savoring on the Ukrainian division in Krakow. Who moved there with her family, like most Ukrainian families who fled the Soviet regime.

Konovalets was killed in Berlin on the personal orders of Stalin.

The family of Stepan Bender and the enemy of the Soviet people remained in the territory of occupied Ukraine. Soviet troops were arrested. On July 41 the Soviet military court sentenced Bender Andrei Mikhailovich to be shot. Sister Oksana, who was arrested together with her father, passed Forty-nine years of camps. In the nineties even filed a request to review the case of father Andrei, he was recognized as a victim of repression and rehabilitated. Marta Maria, another sister of Bendey, died in exile, Alexander and Vasily were tortured in Ausventsevo.

On the 30th of June 1941 the battalion Nachtigal, having put on his German uniforms of the blue-and-yellow ribbon entered the abandoned Chervonnaya Army of Lviv. By noon all strategic objects, including the radio station, had been captured. Together with the Ukrainian nationalists, the German army entered Lvov. While the Germans were busy establishing their authority in the city, Benderevtsi announced the same day the act of revival of the Ukrainian state, became a sausage of a surprise for the Nazis. On the market square, from the balcony, the law read Yaroslav Stitskm. The document survived until our days.

"By the will of the Ukrainian people, the Organizing Committee of the Ukrainian Nationalists announces the restoration of the Ukraine state, for which generations of naming sons of Ukraine laid their heads."

Hitler issued an order to arrest all the leaders and Stytsko, including all party activists, who were mostly shot, as they affected only western Ukraine and could not be of any other use.

Just like that, people from this territory showed everybody that they would never give up the rights.

They always would be western land, Ukraine. Stepan Bender will be forever remembered as a person who fought for the independence of Ukraine and her people, from any enemies. Invaders, starting with a healthy way of life and ending with those who live by war. Fearing that in the future Ukrainians will remember Bender, as a hero who he was in the struggle for real Russia. Not for the Moscow Kingdom so is hidden under the consonance of Russia, immediately ordered the enemy of the people and the accuser.

History crashed into the memory of those who dreamed in those days that once again objected by raising the banner in Ukraine's new struggle for an independent country.

Central Ukraine heroically defended itself from enemies. On the orders of the commander-in-chief from Moscow, the army hastily left the territory of its native land to level the front and protect those most strategically essential people who were vital for building the military strength of the army in the rear. Most of the people in the military, from small to big heroines, fought with invaders. That is why the distant borders of Russia Siberia are one of the largest diasporas of Ukraine and almost all of Russia's elite has Ukrainian roots. It was in those regions that the power of the army was forged for a counter strike. According to statistics, every third in the military was a Ukrainian. Of course, those who were tortured by the regime in the USSR were the same Siberians. They were mostly called political. Politically condemned the first who went as alive counts on the enemy, as soon as it became clear where is the first level. While looking for a beginning level, the enemy was stuck in the battles for Kiev, who knows where.

On July 11, fighting began at the closest lands to the city's [32]. Kiev operation and the Defense of the Kiev fortified district. On September 19, 1941, the 37th Army of the Reds, which defended the city, abandoned it and began to make its way out of the encirclement. On the same day, troops of the 6th German Army entered Kiev. More than 70 days the defense of the city continued.

The efforts of the defenders, together with the 26th (F. Ya. Kostenko) and the 5th Army (MI Potapov), were detained for two months and entangled in grueling position battles in west of Kiev with the 6th Army of the Germans. This allowed in the problematic situation of 1941 to evacuate many industrial enterprises of the city, part of the civilian population and contingents of future recruits [7].

The fighting for Kiev, of course, meant a major tactical success. However, the question of whether this tactical success also had a major strategic significance remains in doubt. Now everything depended on the fact whether the Germans would be able to achieve decisive results even before the onset of winter, perhaps even before the autumn slush period. True, the planned offensive to squeeze Leningrad into a closed ring was already suspended.

The defeat of the South-Western Front opened the way for the enemy to Eastern Ukraine, to the Donbas. The forces of the Southern Front of the Red Army fell into a difficult situation:

+ On October 8 - the 18th Army of the Southern Front was surrounded and lost in the Azov Sea.

+ On October 16 - the Odessa defensive area was abandoned to the enemy.

+ On October 17 - the Donbass is occupied (Taganrog fell).

+ On October 25 - Kharkov was captured.

+ November 2 - the Crimea is held, and Sevastopol is blocked.

+ November 30 - the forces of the Army Group "South" were entrenched on the frontier of the Minus Front.

"We did not even think at the time how correctly, I attributed myself a few years and went to the front. We fought for the right to be all together, we left our home, and sometimes our relatives and left, we felt betrayed when there was an order to retreat, and we were eager to fight. When they took the Crimea and blocked Sevastopol, all of us in the army precisely hated Stalin. He was an answer for how people died there and that we even lost the peninsula. One day I heard about the version that we have to blame someone from people of Ukraine for it, I realized that there is a war in which we are not participants. We have won our own for us for the future of our children and the childhood of our grandchildren; for more, this victory was not enough." My beloved grandfather Sasha, the real hero of the war, the best person that I knew in my life. When I was born, as soon as my mother's older sister arrived, she immediately said, "He will be called Sasha, and now each of the sisters of the oldest son was called Sasha in honor of grandfather Sasha."

The German army has lost more than 100,000 people here. In 1941-1943 in the area of Babi Yar was Syretsky death camp. During the occupation, more than 100 thousand inhabitants of Kiev and prisoners of war were shot here. November 3, 1943 troops of the First Ukrainian Front launched the Kiev offensive operation. November 5, 1943, in the morning the Wehrmacht began withdrawing forces from the city. By the morning of November 6, the capital of Soviet Ukraine Kiev was liberated by the Red Army, 1943.

In the landing, amid a green field and a clear sky, where the fight stopped for five minutes.

"He pulls on the left, pulls, pulls... " (Leszek Titarenko).

"Pierogi are getting cold comrades Pilots... " (Cook).

"With cherries?" (Leszek Titarenko).

"No, with the cottage cheese. " (Cook).

"The commander accomplished the task. " (Sparrows).

"Sit down; what did you see?" (Leszek Titarenko).

"I saw how one with a great smoke, but I did not see how it fell." (Sparrows).

"Not that. " (Leszek Titarenko).

"Can me? " (Alyabyev).

"What did you see?" (Leszek Titarenko).

"From the first nine, two lap-dogs filled, the others left. " (Alyabyev).

"Not that. Vano, what did you see? " (Leszek Titarenko).

"We were putting down by four forks, but we left and got to you. " (Vano).

"I knocked down, I knocked down, comrade Commander. (Ivan Fedorovich).

"Aiaiyai, what have you done?"

"I'll have to call your parents to the director."

"Tomorrow. " (Vano).

"Exactly. " (Alyabyev).

"The exact word knocked down. " (Ivan Fedorovich).

"With fright, Probably." (Sparrows).

"Congratulations on the first victory, but among other things, Ivan Fyodorovich, shoot down enemy aircraft is not a feat. This is the duty of a fighter now, in our everyday life, but what did you see? " (Leszek Titarenko).

"In battle? " (Ivan Fedorovich).

"Well, yes! " (Leszek Titarenko).

"Aaaa... " (Ivan Fedorovich).

The dog scraped.

"Do not tell me." (Leszek Titarenko).

"Hi, Second, let's drink milk."

"Alive, paw cracked? " (Leszek Titarenko).

"10 breaks vomited in the tank, but I do not have scratches. How do you say, Maestro? – Going to be alive!"

"So, what did you see?" How could you not have noticed? Today we fought over by Ukraine. (Leszek Titarenko).

"How would you notice, the same fires, the same roads, the same villages." (Alyabyev).

"Eh no, but the air is different! The sky is blue, and the earth is greener. " (Leszek Titarenko).

"Commander, about the greens in Siberia..." (Alyabyev).

"My dearest friend, why Siberia, come to Bakuriani. Have a look there, see Bakuriani, you will see what's green, what're a mountain." (Vano).

"Have you seen Elesey?" (Alyabyev).

"No, I didn't see. Have you seen Tskhenisthal? " (Vano).

"Let's go ... " Commenting on the conversation of the guys, said Serega.

Too many conversations - laughing.

"Quiet! Lark... " (Serega).

Shot of a missile trigger.

All this has already been, we must all know this, but all that it's our, gentlemen, you can't take away from the people. After all, no matter how it was, we all should stop and forgive each other's everything. Otherwise, it will not end. It is ridiculous and sinful to say to those who are in the grave about what is happening on earth in which something like because we still were one country, were considered one kind of human. We loved the homeland in which they did not distinguish between each other, Russian, Belarus, Kazakh, or Ukrainian the war was swamped when they lived together in the Soviet Union.

No matter where you were born, you could find yourself and live in another revenge of this vast country and as then and now for the whole time of a new sovereign Ukraine. I swear to you that there was not a person that force to speak or write in the language to which he or she wouldn't like. The lays that are sown is already so bored that the patience of the chapel does not find in absurdity those conversations.

Malice takes and resentment for what was and what we now have, we all the same there and here. No, we do not want to be alone with you in this country. We do not need it. We need a rest and not even hear about you, but still, it's a history, and how can you forget it? People's account of those who were driven in the back by dictators, bastards and corrupt skins, now you are trying to praise him. You know yourself who they were, those who led us all our lives. What we have now it is not better, but believe, they will not be there for too long more. I dream only about one thing brother and sister for all of us that the sun and the wind of the peaceful sky should be felt above our heads.

In fact, at that time all the people were got together, realizing that it would be impossible to defeat this communist power and the fascists. Everyone believed and as everyone now understands and still choose less evil between two of them, even when, on the orders of Stavka, they shot in the back. If they stopped at the attack or would run back. Victory at any cost for Stalin was the main thing, and in this context, it will be tricky to say that in reality, the losses of our army should be two times smaller.

The main crime of this war in our rear was Comrade Stalin. The level of sarcasm in the Words about Comrade Stalin is off the scale. Also, that went into battle with each other's cartridges with a rifle breaking into pairs, the very principle of attack was groundless now when the army's actions should be sharpened on the tactics of defense and held back by the enemy. It was during the retreat that the best forces of the regiment were lost. The first die the best and believe; they were running themselves, they didn't need to be fallow in case they want to run back. Of course, this entire war created those people who, in their belief in humanity. The fight for the motherland was so pure in their souls after what they had seen. They passed that they dreamed only of one thing: to come back later and build one big world that would be fair and even for all people on the Earth.

All this sounds like this, but imagine the terrible battlefield - this is the worst thing. "You are all fleas, and the installation of Katyusha over the trench is being swept up by volleys, the sea of volleys, and the commander is shouting into battle!"

My other grandfather, whom I, unfortunately, did not know, as many others, even when they returned, could not regain themselves in a healthy life. After all the horror that they saw that they had passed personally. Do you even understand what our people went through? What tragedy and destruction in this war, at least because it was all on our territory and what happened to each family? As we have preserved ourselves and are trying to do something with faith in a better life. By remembering our ancestors, we are trying to change something in Ukraine. It's a pity we do not have the right people some adherents, as it was seen after the Orange Revolution. This was a chance to start over again, although I am sure that everyone must first start with themselves.

This power carries with it emptiness and deception, as in Russia, and the belief in one person as a national idea in Russia is generally marasmus for zombified people with TVs. The replacement of the notion of life and what is happening. We believed in the USSR in a system that should work for generations ahead, naive if it was built on the horrors that the Stalinists were creating. Although because of it could not stand for too long. Only voluntarily and in modern realities, we should make the same leap in the social and political sense, as in scientific and technological progress. All these lessons of history are an integral part of the reality of the present moment of our time. For the sake of just one moment, like this, when I woke up in the morning and was shocked by what happened at night.

Everything, as always, the students went out to the square to speak out, against. It was still like that for us, for generations and centuries. This time, as already happened before. They were taken into the ring and those who joined the students because people will always come out and support even a small rally.

3:30 There were only a few hundred peaceful protesters who harmoniously merged with the rhythm of the life of the city center.

4:00 The people surrounded the monument on its small hills, began to sing together the Ukrainian anthem while the square along with the protesters surrounded about 2,000 armed with unique means of fighters "Berkut" and said, "Dear citizens request to liberate the territory of the Independence Square workers will work here "as soon as this zakli came out, the soldiers of the" Golden Eagle "did not hear the voices of the people who chanted " the police with the people." " The police with the people." The police with the people, "Militia and the people " native "heard only have batons, explosive packages were thrown to the ground with the people of Independence pedestal and crushed underfoot. Moreover, on the way to the square, people are already beginning to beat "Shame," "Shame," "Shame," "Shame," "Shame," "Shame."

4:15 Wriggling people are jumping in different directions, trying to break through the ring, hear the abusive words of law enforcement officers when they beat people with all the hatred that they have. The desperate cry of a man pierces the air. They began to hit people, closer to the monument. A woman from the crowd, "Do you have a conscience?" The man, "What are you doing?" Student, "For what?"

Try not to let each other to fall, and helping to rise, in the air the screeching of girls, and heart-rending calls to stop. Do not regret truncheons of non-humans, even the elderly. You can hear blows to the unprotected bodies and limbs of people. Some people who are behind the ring, were already able to escape, crying seeing how the surrounding protesters are mercilessly struck. Here the girl was pulled unconscious on the asphalt. This horror is accompanied by a screech of bulls this other helpless person.

People start chanting together "Shame", "Shame", "Shame", "Shame", "Shame", "Shame"...

4:30 Everyone is taken out of the square, some are still being hit, one hears as a little girl chants, "heroes do not die; heroes do not die; heroes do not die; heroes do not die; heroes do not die..."

4:45 A small servant from the St. Michael's Cathedral, is near, everyone who managed to escape from the square, took with him to prevent them from catching and hiding from the search for special employees. Cleaning the territory of the square, quarters of the gates, for some reason the telephone the connection did not work.

Nobody expected what happened next.

18:00 On November 30, Mikhailovskaya Square, above Independence Square in Kiev, Ukraine, hundreds of thousands of people gathered to protest government crimes and beating students.

An incredible number of people flooded the Mikhailovsky Square, with a rally, with calls, "Country Get up." At the same time, rallies are held all over the country in support of Kiev, the largest in Lviv, Kharkov and Zaporozhye.

"I realized at that moment that it was starting something new. That now the reality begins, to live and fight and I have found myself because this is a chance, another chance for all of us. People themselves came out just normal Kiev people, they went in other cities this evening too, after what happened yesterday. Here is no politicians or PR here is only we, Ukrainian people are ready to stand against and say our official word. If only all these freaks and parasites that are at war with each other in power we can win, if not all at once, then later, but achieved our goals. Perfect time, I returned home. "

* "Hello everyone - this is Svetoslav Vokarchuk, who gives an interview on a mobile phone."

"In fact, despite what is happening not just in Ukraine, but somewhere deep in my heart, Pawnee optimism. I want to use the phrase of Nitsha, " Everything that does not kill us makes us stronger. " and that we can come out strong, tolerant, confident and successful from this situation to the future, and made sure that such things never happened again - I believe in Us.

* "When did you go to the square for the first time?"

* "As a simple person I came out to people right away in the first days, it was interesting for me to feel this spirit. The sincerity struck me, especially the students went to Maidan - it was, so you know. It was somehow very, very honestly. There was some very positive drive; well, I decided to address the students."

* "We talked, as they called on the sidelines. They speak to them, and they asked to say something public, and those conversations that we were talking about values, I said on the stage on Thursday.

I was far from discussing with them politically. Now, I do not think about politics too, but what happened in the morning is no longer politics; it's some kind, among the unimaginable horror.

It's impossible to remain silent about this it's obvious. I would like us to live in a country in which it will never happen again."

* "Did you have any doubts, go out or not?"

* "No, actually look - I'll tell the truth - I'm skeptical of being so far, I have... Such a thing as it's called? Immunity to political events, I would not want to participate, to call on people with my voice and authority: support these, support those."

Firstly, Ukrainian politics is very complex and unpredictable. Secondly, I'm now engaged in creativity, and at the moment, at this time, I was happy that I'm in love, but there is. There are moments when you cannot remain silent; You just cannot. It does not matter. This is about politics.

You misunderstand it's about our future for many years to come, so it's different things if it would be about politics. There would not be all these people, and I would not be there. I can say - it might look like abstinence from an answer, but it's all so complicated now and not predictable. I do not want to give any forecasts now. I hope, "THAT'S ALL WILL BE OKAY."

November 30, 19:30 Ukraine, Kiev, studio 1 + 1, live broadcast. This is one of the interviews with a person who is trying to do something for people. Ruslana has always been in grief and glory in our new history / Not so honest as she.

* "Also this is Ruslana Lozhichko's call for our Euro symbol, our person, who has already conquered all Europe at Eurovision Song Contest. Thanked you for your courage, for your indifference and that you took part in our program."

* "Thanks, hold on we'll win!"

Others replaced some events, everything was very fast, understanding the mood of the people, the opposition and the forces are different. Probably certainly supported by all people, and most important from this moment, people from all over Kiev are scrambling every evening to stand together for several hours in support of changes in Ukraine. It becomes clear that this is not a meeting of one day. They installed a stage where people can perform, and everyday patriots from all over the country go to Kiev to support protest and change. Every day more and more famous people and foreign countries from all over the world come here. The authorities decided to ignore the process of what is happening likely. The people present at negotiations with the same disgusting faces. People who can, especially students, understand the historical moment and spend the days on Independence day in the daytime and the evening. Yesterday the first snow began, we hope winter will not be severe, we need to stand out here in the cold in the square and demand a change in 12/01/2013.

Abandoned by law enforcers, Maidan was flooded with people from the very morning blocking traffic along the central street of the capital.

A group of people wearing masks and with baseball bats and metal Tsipko, grabbing one of the tractors that stood among other equipment on Maidan for the installation of a Christmas tree. This went straight to the soldiers of the internal troops, who were further blocking Bankovaya street, to protect the presidential administration, but at the last moment, they were hardly stopped by other protesters.

The leader of the group "TAR-TAK" Sashko Polozhinsky called from the very bucket, "Now, we will tinker. As a result, the top will remain the same. If we want the revolution, we need to attract people, not pushing them out."

The deputy Petro Poroshenko tried to calm down the people, and the policy was dropped from the geyser and the guard were cut with a knife.

When the provocateurs declined, and the conflict seemed to come to its logical conclusion, the particular army went on the attack. They beat everyone without any human sense. When the military retreated, they were stoned. Young men in black masks were standing behind their backs. Some politicians still persuade people to calm down and call for peaceful protest.

For the first time, people learn about other protesters who provoke and are mercenaries of power, they start to call "carcasses."

By the evening, tens of thousands of people gathered in the square, despite the incredible cold, to the glory, honor, and dignity of their native country and against the bandit regime.

People for the first time wear protective equipment from cudgels.

12/04/2013 From the east of the country "carcasses" go to the capital, which is already up to five thousand in the Mariinsky park, under the guise of "Berkut."

Every day more and more famous people and foreign countries from all over the world come here. The authorities decided to ignore the process of what is happening likely. The people present at negotiations with the same disgusting faces. People who can, especially students, understand the historical moment and spend the days on Independence Day in the daytime and the evening. Yesterday the first snow began, we hope winter will not be severe, we need to stand out here in the cold in the square and demand a change.

On December 1, 2013, abandoned by law enforcers, Maidan was flooded with people from the very morning blocking traffic along the central street of the capital.

A group of people wearing masks and with baseball bats and metal Tsipko, grabbing one of the tractors that stood among other equipment on Maidan for the installation of a Christmas tree. They went straight to the soldiers of the internal troops. The soldiers were further blocking Bankovaya street, to protect the presidential administration, but at the last moment, they were hardly stopped by other protesters.

The leader of the group "TAR-TAK" Sashko Polozhinsky called from the very bucket: "Now, we will tinker, and as a result, the top will remain the same. If we want the revolution, we need to attract people, not pushing them out..."

The deputy Petro Poroshenko tried to calm down the people, and the policy was dropped from the geyser and the guard were cut with a knife.

When the provocateurs declined, and the conflict seemed to come to its logical conclusion, the particular army went on the attack. They beat everyone without any human sense. When the military retreated, they were stoned. Young men in black masks were standing behind their backs. Some politicians still persuade people to calm down and call for peaceful protest.

For the first time, people learn about other protesters who provoke and are mercenaries of power, they start to call "carcasses."

By the evening, tens of thousands of people gathered in the square, despite the incredible cold, to the glory, honor, and dignity of their native country and against the bandit regime.

People for the first time wear protective equipment from cudgels.

On December 4, 2013, from the east of the country "carcasses" go to the capital, which is already up to five thousand in the Mariinsky park, under the guise of "Berkut."

Prime Minister of Ukraine, declares: "We have enough power to forces you all, to stop what is going on."

12/8/2013 On December 8, 2013, in Russia, Moscow on Telechannel RUSSIA 1 in the weekly news.

"And now there is already a battle, that peacefully goes to Europe, but the police do not let him in, here's another euro integrator, and also with a chain." (He starts to babble, in contrast to the replica before, with an agreeable and calm voice) "The picture was taken during the attempted storming of the presidential administration in Kiev, even before the protesters on the Maidan began to disperse." The host again switched to a calm tone. "Let's look at the photo in more detail. Helmets of policemen, young guys, crouch under a whistling chain, in front of them, "crazy man," confident in its, all impunity.

Now, the Ukrainian street appellation appeals for help to the US, saying the action was peaceful, but we were offended. I'm sure that if there were such a thing in America, "a crazy man with a chain," the police officers would shoot straight away, but for Kiev, it's okay. From Americans and enlightened Europe, is it? "(The last words were said with intonation, cynicism, and surprise.)" But here in my hands, the protective "helmet" of the Ukrainian soldier of the internal troops who were, in that very line, defending the office of the president of Ukraine. The "helmet" that's literally along the cut the very chain from that man, what happened with a head is unknown, the visor is broken, that was a beginning.

"In any country in the world, the storming of the presidential administration would be qualified as an attempt to seize government power. I already hear people talking about provocateurs, but there are always provocateurs in the course of mass actions if leaders declare peaceful protest. Then they must control provocateurs. If they do not control them, then provocations are laid in the script, then the rally is no longer peaceful." (The video shows video fragments, "carcasses" with a chain, collisions on Belkovsky Street with a tractor and people with internal troops).

"Then, it is necessary to be ready and to force repulse; it is inevitable. It is possible that the reaction will seem excessive..." (The words are already mentioned under the video of the dispersal of the Maidan on the night of November 30, a day earlier).

"...it will hurt, and blood will flow, then this blood will flood the screens of the TVs of the whole world, very quickly, but maybe this was the plan. But for those who developed it, the blood is the paint? -

It seems, yes. Because after all, at first the policeman got hard, provoked, maimed and strangled with gas... " (again the video from 1st-2nd December).

"... and then, the protest leaders called to Maidan, the poor students. This left them cynically there without any protection, like a victim provided for by political technology. Under the script, we need "blood" the complete construction of the riots was built in such a way that "blood" will spill, and it dropped.

Prehistory of the "spilled blood" on the world's screens is not existed, smoothly orchestrated. If so, I dare to suggest that on the globe screens a joint production, with the west, in the movie it is called "co- production", then the winged one is recalled. "it does not matter how they vote, the main thing is how they think", if paraphrased, it does not matter how it happened. It is essential to show. Well, here the blood is shown on Maidan, without prehistory. Then they refer to this picture.

"The whole world looks at Ukraine..." says in Kiev Assistant Secretary of United States Victoria Nuland, "... now the government will go either to meet the interests of people. Then the country can face chaos and violence". The interests of the people here are just a bow. The main thing is the promise of chaos and violence. It is a direct threat. If we remember that the American embassy in Kiev since summer conducts training for bloggers under the program "Techcamp." If you count the money that Americans have always poured into Ukraine, to make Ukraine more against to Russia, then Nuland's words are NOT an accident.

How much neglect in this word! It seems that the words are addressed to a country whose days are finished.

During the events at Taksim Square in Stubul, there were also massive pro-European actions against the creeping Islamization, in which Erdogan's accusers. And also cruel reprisals. But nothing disrespectful to a robust Turkey Victoria Nuland of the United States did not allow herself. Neither threats nor pathos predictions of "chaos and violence" Turkey did not have. In the address of Ukraine, it means you can. Does the smell of provoked blood so intoxicating and the anticipation of even greater prey make the diplomat look like a crow?

Or the German foreign minister Guido Westerwelle. For the same-sex married Westerwelle meeting on the Maidan with brothers, Klitschko was a bright event. Warmed, or overheated by bodies of heavyweights, the minister in Kiev said: "Ukraine should be on board with Europe because we have many things to share: common history and common culture, common values."

The values of LGBT people in the EU are a favorite. But all this is on the Maidan! This is already a significant provocation.

And what is this, Maidan? A small point on the body of Ukraine. If you burn it with a soldering iron, it will hurt. But if you make all the political technologies competently - create a point of overheating, then show it through the Magnifying glass (television and the Internet - the perfect optics) and create the impression that the whole country is now all that same, it can turn out to be fatal.

12/11/2013

On Mayday December 11, 2013, about ten thousand protesters gathered, people who heard about the plans of the authorities to clean up the Maidan continued to walk to the center of the capital.

From the stage Ruslana's voice could be heard:

-"Berkut, please stop, you go against ordinary people. You hear my voice. Please stop, ordinary people, ask you, singers, artists, musicians, standing on the stage, please do not do this. Berkut does not work the crimes of orders; please do not crush ordinary people, you will regret it tomorrow, you will apologize next week. Do not make a mistake now. This is a simple human mistake, don't do it.

You are not military now. There are no strategic objects here. People without guns are standing, simple girls and the young man, don't. Don't follow!

At this time around the world, a picture is broadcast from the Maidan, where people ask for help".

An incredible number of people on the night square begins to chant, "Serve the people of Ukraine... serve the people of Ukraine." At dawn, the voice of the people with another attack of exceptional employees, already chanted: "shit, shame, disgrace, shame... we stand, we stand." On the stage, the clergymen continue to read the prayer service. At dawn, all the Mayday, keeping the positions and defending the barricades after the storming of the military and those "carcasses", sang the Anthem of Ukraine. It becomes clear that we cannot merely be stopped, and we survived this night and will survive more.

On December 12, 2013, the authorities mobilized particular employees.

"To alert the subjects of the fight against terrorism in the territory of the Kiev region."

Meanwhile, in Strasbourg, excessive use of force against protesters was condemned, power.

The opposition was called for negotiations. The assembly was shown Ukrainian flags, which they brought with them in support of the Ukrainian people.

In Ukraine, as an institution, a pro-government meeting is held with the paid people and traitors of the Ukrainian people. As in the election for the presidency of Ukraine Yanukovych, and not the election of Vitali Klitschko, the national hero of sports of Ukraine, as mayor of Kiev.

Statement from Stefana Fule:

"The words and actions of the president and the government, according to the agreement. In the future, diverge, their arguments have nothing to do with the realities."

The opposition said it expects the president to resign from the government.

Yanukovych again met with Putin and agreed on the cheap gas and a loan of $ 13 billion. Putin said that this is not connected with the proposal of Ukraine's accession to the Customs Union.

On Decemeber 14, 2013 21:30 Independence Square Kiev Ukraine.

On the stage behind the back of the leader of Maidan Evgeny Nishchuk, you can see a portrait of Taras Shevchenko. The sea of people filled the Maidan, in frost, the Ocean filled the people, which echoes, "Glory to Ukraine," "Glory to Heroes," "Glory to Ukraine," "Glory to Heroes."

"The beautiful sea of Ukrainian people is a big Ocean - it's a group, Ocean of Elzi."

On the stage, there appears the soloist of the group Okean Elzy Sviatoslav Vokarchuk,

"Good evening Maidan, good evening Kiev, good evening of Ukraine."

I see before. Honestly, I do not see where people end. I understand that this is our record.

We went to it for a long time and finally came, grateful that you are all here with us today, we are very, very pleased.

A couple of words, "I" would like to say why "We" are standing on this stage right now. We stand on this stage. We dedicate this speech today, to all those guys who were ruthlessly beaten on Saturday night, who were in no way guilty. The footage with which flew around the whole the world is an atrocity, for them and their sake families and their friends, for the sake of those who stood here on Sunday who was completely innocent people. Among whom was our top manager, were taken away, without any explanation and put in jail. We stand here for those people from The east, from the west, for the people who are now supporting European integration. Even for the sake of those people who are possible against it, but for those people who are waiting for how much time from the power of justice. That they are heard, for the sake of those people who do not understand why the courts release the perpetrators of the murders of downed people guilty of murder while being under the influence of alcohol intoxicated by the children of officials and majors. They release them, while not guilty people are imprisoned without trial. For the sake of those people who are waiting for justice from power. On the one side of the Dnieper and the other. It unites us, not politics joinus. "We" want us to be heard. "We" want "our" to be dignified, we want our freedom to be perceived as an obvious thing and do not tell "Us" every day of the figures and the economy at a time when. Not innocent people, absolutely for nothing, as always in the end, recently, answer. I would like so each of us understands that this is Our country and it's each of us. I, my Friends on the stage, each of you who stand here. We answer for the country, if politicians do not hear us, then We use that single article of the Constitution that says, "All power in the country belongs to the people. And I want you to remember it. This peaceful protest will surely bring us to our goal. And each of us will feel that We are free and worthy, and Our Country is free and dignified, grateful to You."

Get up!

Get up!

Drink tea with milk,

Pray on a warm shower!

Millions of new hearts

Are sleeping without you today!

Demand more! (Several times)

....

And outside behind the window is almost spring and my God

....

The people chant: "Well done, well done, well done..."

....

Thank you for your support and your friendship.

"If you once told me

Become your boat,

If only once, I would have taken you

And floated to the freedom..."

People on phones switched on flashlights and in the modern language of the latest technology, called the whole world to peace.

On the Maidan, that evening, two hundred thousand people gathered. The ocean sang only nine songs, and these moments will remain in the memory of people for life, even then it was understood by everyone. We every day create history, carrying justice, peace, and honesty, competing with evil and injustice, and these video frames our life together with you saw the whole world. We stretched out our hands to heaven, urging all of humanity to join us and become one, for peace in the entire world and the prosperity of good.

On December 12, 19, 2013 Yanukovych signs the law on the release of all those who arrested, after which they still release not all of them.

At the end of 2013, Donetsk there are actions in support of the Euro-Maidan.

On December 22, 2013, Mazurenko Pavel Anatolyevich Ukrainian from the Zhitomir region. On the evening of December 18, 2013, on the way home, in the Svyatoshinsky district near the shopping center

"Kvadrat," at he, was beaten by employees of the Berkut (according to other sources - Chop). On December 21, went to the hospital, where a concussion was recorded, died the next day. The official conclusion of forensic medical examination is bilateral pleuropneumonia.

On December 25, 13, people from Euro-Maidan continue to hunt down and threaten with reprisals, one of the journalists is catching up on the road and being beaten very hard.

In another day show New Year's release of the studio "cvartal 95" December 31, 2012, Palace of Ukraine city of Kiev and tens of millions of people on TV screens.

Yesterday I had a beautiful dream

The whole Council was burnt.

All Ukraine is celebrating the new year. We are all in the hopes that everything is still ahead, although the authorities are silent. The meeting is frozen. By the fact that they came to Sofia's Square, everything was transferred to Maidan already a long time ago. The opposition established the stage and registering an application for holding rallies. People from all over the country support the Maidan. The hope is smoldering in hot coals.

We met with my best friend Zhenya and his girlfriend and bought various medicines and products for Maidan. Activists have already even hung out lists on the internet. What is needed first and what is missing. We walked with full packages along Lesia Ukrainka Avenue, snow was falling from the sky and fastened under the shoes. The time when everybody was wearing black has passed already for a long time. My jacket was green, Zhenena-yellow, and Veronica red. The smell of winter gave way to the scent of Maidan, -burnt tires and food cooked on the fire, when we approached the KMDA (Kiev city state administration), that on Khreshchatyk.

On January 6, 2014, a monument to Lenin overthrown in Zhytomyr region. Despite the frantic cold, all these days, people continue to gather for peaceful protests.

On January 1, 2014, people who destroyed the monument to Lenin in Boryspil were convicted for six years. People began to rally against such a decision.

On January 16, 2014, The law on extremism:

These legislative acts, in the opinion of most experts, limited the rights of citizens, gave the state authorities more considerable discretion in punishing participants in protest actions. Aimed to criminalize the opposition and civil society. They were signed by Yanukovych the next morning.

Banditska authorities said that laws on those who voted with a simple show of hands are not a subject for cancellation.

Brussels, in turn, said that these laws make people concern.

The first deputies began to form the mandates of the pro-government faction.

There is the most massive vote on the square in the new year, against criminal laws. On which law enforcement officers use gas and light grenades. People of Maidan and activists of Kiev rushed to defend their owns, Vitali Klitschko in the thick of events tried very hard to translate everything into a peaceful channel, standing out for his large structured bodies. Quick one after another exported the victims from the scene.

In the Verkhovna Rada in the meantime, again, with a simple show of hands, another ten laws are passed. Practically the new reality of the country in which:

- A convoy of more than five cars is a crime.

- To be at the rally in a mask is a crime.

- Establish a tent, a scene, and sound evil.

- Blocking personal property or not respectfully speaking about a judge is a criminal offense.

- All public associations financed from abroad must be called foreign agents

- Internet space will be limited.

This stop-frame records that for the bill on the introduction of the dictatorship, 118-120

Deputies voted. Lesja Orobets.

"It's a joke in 3-5 seconds, but that's how long it took to vote, to count all these hands in such a crowd, but where did 235 get there or according to the website of the Verkhovna Rada of Ukraine 239?"

Orobets is surprised. Meanwhile, a group of young activists of the Maidan decided to go ahead.

Block the Verkhovna Rada to seek the abolition of extremist laws. Barricades of law enforcement officers stood in their way. Some politicians of the opposition authorities began to disavow and tried to appeal only to peaceful protest. On the street Grushevsky, bilateral attacks began, where these areas are used stones and paving stones with Molotov cocktails. Which law enforcement officers meet with rubber bullets and metal checkers of light and noise grenades. During the night of the confrontations, the ambulance took away about two hundred wounded. In the morning the protesters suspended active operations but continuously kept the "Berkut" in suspense, knocking on empty barrels with sticks. As if in drums, as in the old Cossack times, in revolts in Ukraine. From specialized equipment "take," almost nothing left.

The head of the department of mass events of the Ministry of Internal Affairs of Ukraine: "... at times the section of committing a group attack threatening the health and life of law enforcement officers, they can even shoot firearms." About twenty offenders are detained; they can receive up to 15 years of imprisonment."

By the evening, practical actions began again on both sides. The demonstrators are attacking a huge number of fireworks that burst loudly and injure the servants of our enemy; here is a mixture of Molotov cock calves and they instantly ignite like Christmas trees.

The politicians stated:

"Most people who are there are acting on their own, those who come here - we provide medical care, we can help, but people act independently."

Under the exclamations "Glory to Ukraine" - "Heroes of Glory," the protesters continued to defend the peaceful protest, to fight, on the fifth day of confrontation suddenly three clergymen with Christ appear between the parties, the battle stops, and ordinary people for barricades, which activists start chanting further " the police with the people, the police with the people, the police with the people, the police with the people. "The first does not stand the siloviki begin to knock and speak in the loudspeaker to stifle the voice of priests praying and call for peace.

On the night Kiev continues raids "titoshok," which are trying to stop the heroes of our time auto-Maydanovs.

01/22/2014 6:00 in Kiev.

During the truce in the street Grushevsky, three shots: one in the sleep artery, the other in the left lung, the third in the head - injuries were incompatible with life. The fate of Sergei Negoyan was broken. On Mayday He was on December 8, every night guarded the barricades, stood with tens of thousands of people on the current Maidan, even then from a bird's-eye view, God could see his pure and peaceful soul. In a day he chopped wood and recited T. Shevchenko.

Beyond the mountains, mountains,

Sown with grief, blood is poured.

From time immemorial Prometheus

There the eagle punishes,

Whichever God's day chops out the ribs

And the heart breaks.

Breaks, but does not drink

Living blood -

Again and again, comes alive

And she laughs again.

Our soul does not die,

Do not kill will.

And I'm not sick of padding

At the bottom of the sea, there is a field.

Does not scent a living soul

And the words of the living.

He will not bear the glory of God,

Great God.

A twenty-year-old young man with a sign (the voice of the people SAYS GOD), tied with the flag of Armenia. On Maidan, he turned the attention of many activists. "This guy I loved as a son - such a bright man." The artist, Boris Egizaryan was struck by the sincere Ukrainian language of Sergei. "It's a soul, it's been tormented, the child is a pure heart, he was such that he stands up for everyone, His cock killed, and he stands for everyone - He died, what would that prove anything... that there is no justice.

"This is unfair, as Ukraine is not allowed to enter Europe ...? Ukraine is a European country."

After the situation in Ukraine was settled, Sergei Nigoyan dreamed of traveling to Armenia, in his historical homeland, He was never.

And to your glory, the blue mountains,

The ice is shrouded in ice.

And to you, knights great,

God is not forgotten.

Fight - probate!

God helps you!

You are right; your glory is for you

And the holy will!

The body without signs of forcible death, but with bundled scotch tape and a pack on its head, was seen by foresters near the village of Gnedin, Borispilsky district.

The activist of the EuroMaidan, who was abducted yesterday from the hospital, Igor Lutsenko, who was found, pointed precisely to these regions, where he was taken out.

"In the forest, we were dragged out of the bus, at first, we were interrogated together with elements of violence, and then they stretched out us, to the ends of the forest, I just heard that they were torturing Yuri, and not me, because he turned out to be a Lvivian. They do not understand anything about the Maidan; they think that people are bought, they wanted to know how much, it's all worth it, how much "They" pay to the US."

Yuri Tarasovich Verbitsky (August 25, 1963, in Lviv - on January 21 or 22, 2014, near Gnedin village, Borispol district, Kiev region) - Hero of Ukraine, seismologist, candidate of science. The son of Ukrainian geophysicist Taras Verbitsky, brother of the seismologist Sergei Verbitsky. The activist of Euro-Majdan; was kidnapped along with Igor Lutsenko by unknown persons on January 21, 2014 and killed after torture.

Quietly carried to the ambulance under the hymn of Ukraine, that day was lost on Maidan, another glorious defender of Ukraine - Belorussian Zhiznevsky Mikhail Mikhailovich. He was killed on January 22, 2014, during clashes on Grushevsky Street. He received a through a wound in the heart of a bullet from the special gun Fort-500; such weapons in the Ministry of Internal Affairs are used to damage the engines of cars. Under the song that He first heard on Maidney and followed him off into a mad way.

Duckling floats on Titan – we all know what that means now !!!

January 22, 2014. Entry TSN.14: 00 In the studio, Alexander Zagorodni.

"On the fact of the death of two people on Grševsky, investigators of the department of the Pechersk militia department instituted criminal proceedings under the premeditated murder, as reported by the Website of the Ministry of Internal Affairs of Ukraine, investigators from the court-medical experts, find out how the circumstances and nature of injuries and injuries to the dead. Meanwhile, the Prime Minister of Ukraine - Mykola Azarov expressed his vision of the events in the center of the capital over the past few days, he sympathizes with the wounded on both sides of the barricades, notes that the law enforcers on Grushevsky do not have firearms and believes that the purpose of the opposition leaders are to provoke the authorities to use force ".

"Those who are interested in these disorders, or call peaceful protestgulyavlyamy, and rally protesters.

It's malicious people who will respond to floods for their actions, as an example the Minister of Ukraine officially declare that the victims, who are already on the level of guilt, on the conscience and responsibility of the organizers. Individual participants in the mass I demand that the law enforcement agencies thoroughly and resolutely investigate this crime. Most importantly, do everything possible to prevent them from happening again."

On January 25, 2013, as a sign of support for people on the Maidan, dignity, and fight against bandit authority, most regional administrations were captured or were in a state of assault. By people on the ground. February 18, 2014, to stop, the attacks of special appointees who do not have time to run back to the square quickly are falling. They are severely beaten and bullied. On the big barricade on Maidan where the activists from Hrushevsky hid, sent an armored personnel carrier, which caught fire at once, for the joy of everyone, from cocktails and could not even break the barricade.

The protesters for the first-time light tires, the smoke trunk goes towards wicked law enforcers enclosing criminal laws. They choke on and cough, moving to their initial positions. God is on our side.

A lot of wounded people are from grenades and shotguns.

"It's amazing; they talked with us for 67 minutes and did not give us a chance to ask questions and share our views. We read your laws, but we also consider the different conditions under which they were adopted. As well as the deeply politicized context of the speech, not only is it about the letter of the law. Moreover, I cannot but note that neither of you in the morning, we heard a single word of regret that the death of two people last night", said the German ambassador.

After the official address, the ambassadors of Great Britain, Germany, and France received only laughter and the opportunity to make an appointment. Where they had already recorded many times.

Millions of people say, "here it is," on the news, everyone was seized, a pain in the heart and anger at the devilish actions of this power.

"The US Embassy is shocked by the death of protesters in Kiev. We condemn the violence that occurs on the streets of Kiev and call on all parties to an immediate settlement of the situation.

The growing tension in the country is the first consequence of the Ukrainian government's refusal to establish a dialogue and adoption of anti-democratic legislation on 16 January.

We also condemn the targeted use of force against the journalists by the Ukrainian authorities about thirty cases, starting from January 19. And we condemn the violence of unofficial bandits and groups known as "titles" against peaceful demonstrators and journalists."

"We are ready to intensify our worldwide cooperation overtime with the Supreme Rada, with the EU, various factions that are ready to build up the Russian-Ukrainian partnership.

We want to say decisive comments today. Those Western politicians who interfere in the Ukrainian cause and led them to stop facilitating the escalation of the conflict immediately, "L. Slutsky hurriedly says with stumbles.

"This is a classic color revolution that is complemented by acts of vandalism and violence. We must perfectly understand that if we do not conclude, this is our future."

Independence Square.

As pomegranates are torn to the pear and heard on Maidan, now it resembles a disturbed anthill.

Men and women knock down the ice, collect snow, and strengthen barricades. Rubber tires that burn on Grushevsky take them out of here. Carry them to the blockade, each with several hundred defenders in armor. The attack here is planned to reflect with stones, for the sake of which the pavement is broken. Men are concentrated but not talkative, but women remember the victims without restraining their emotions.

February 19, 2014, Ukraine Kiev.

The entry into Kiev is limited, seven protesters and two militiamen have already died. The term of the ultimatum of power, about the release of the protesters of the Maidan, was issued. By lunchtime, there were three hundred wounded. The metropolitan was stopped, the battles took on the most mass confrontations and brutal beating of the square, which is surrounded. Individual members of the armed forces armed with firearms, light with grenade grenades. The police seize the footage from the journalists beating the cameras. Before the Maidan, two armored vehicles with weapons and 25 tons of mini busses of the same type were recovered. All the Alpha group, hammered by special appointees, who were in ammunition and with Kalashnikov assault rifles. Up to the square, three water cannons are straightened up at the point-new range and water people in this terrible frost and try to extinguish the flames. There is almost nothing to breathe on the barricades. People sing the anthem of Ukraine.

The authorities are announcing the beginning of an anti-terrorist operation. The ambulance one after another departs from the Maidan with the wounded. The tents were lit, and a large number of wounded, who are delayed in time, and replaced by new defenders. Do not change their resolve on the Maidan, people are ready to face the enemy face to face. The house of trade unions has lighted up.

The account of the victims goes to thousands, and the dead are already up to a hundred this night, which the heroes of Ukraine have stood.

9:30 "We need doctors! A lot of wounded, "says European on Twitter.

9:39 Many ambulances gathered at Mikhailovskaya Square.

9:40 The security forces retreat from the Council; the protesters are storming. The correspondent of "LIGABusinessInform reports this."

9:47 On the Maidan, the siloviki are expected to attack from Grushevsky and Institutskaya. On the stage, they say that a sniper is sitting at the October Palace. Several hundreds of siloviks descend from the side of the Cabinet. They are much more numerous than the protesters, "the correspondent of" Public TV "assures.

9:48 am New groups of captured militiamen are constantly leading to the Independence Square, reports "Espresso.TV". Mostly they are BB fighters. On Grushevsky, the negotiators are nominated by the Maidanovites. There is information that the soldiers are ready to appear in large numbers and require guarantees of their security.

10:00 "Fatherland" states that law enforcement officers fired from firearms protesters against the authorities from the roof of the Kiev Conservatory. This is stated in the press service of the party concerning the information of the headquarters of the national resistance.

10:01 In the Ukrainian house and the October Palace are now fighters "Berkut." This was reported in Twitter "Fatherland." In the October Palace, the siloviki are firing machine guns, "says Espreso.TV

10:02 Dozens of internal troops from Hrushevsky Street surrendered to self-defense Euro-Ladies, the correspondent of RBC-Ukraine reports. They surrender under security guarantees. Self-defense Maidan makes them a corridor through the crowd and tries to make sure that they do not get beaten. The men go from Hrushevsky through the European square to the Maidan. Totally as of 10:05 several dozens of WW fighters appeared.

On Institutskaya Street, intense fighting continues between self-defense of the Maidan and the Berkut.

10:08 titles and eagles go with one column, "writes EuroMeidan on Twitter.

10:11 Members of the Right Sector organization deny the truce between the authorities and activists and are ready to continue the offensive. About this on his page on Facebook, the leader of the movement, Dmitry Yarosh wrote.

11:50 According to Forbes sources, the internal troops are brought to full combat readiness.

Noon in social networks, there was information that more than ten people died from sniper bullets on the Independence Square. As reported on its page in Facebook, Honored Doctor of Ukraine and a civil activist Olga Bogomolets, only in the last hour shot targets killed 13 people. Their bodies are now in the hotel "Ukraine."

12:15 The Interior Ministry denied the information about the mass transfer of fighters to the side of the protesters. "All this nothing more than rumors, which are deliberately distributed by the participants in the riots," the press service of the ministry said.

14:00 As of 12.00 on February 20, 2014, since February 18, 35 people have died in the center of Kiev since the beginning of the clashes. This was reported by the press service of the Ministry of Health of Ukraine.

16:00 "In the clashes in Kiev on February 20, according to preliminary information at 15.20, more than 60 people were killed", said the head of the medical service of the National Resistance Headquarters, People's Deputy of Ukraine from the Svoboda HH Sviatoslav Khanenko.

16:15 The Vice-Speaker of the Verkhovna Rada Ruslan Koshulinsky opened the session of the Verkhovna Rada. After the opening of the Council, a one-hour break was announced at once. The quorum is not yet in the parliament; according to journalists, there are about two hundred people's deputies in the parliament. The break is announced to gather more people's deputies. In the parliament, there are almost no people's deputies from the PR and CPU.

17:16 The Ministry of Internal Affairs says that the protesters captured about 70 WW fighters. "To free the captured colleagues. The police have the right to use weapons," the ministry said in a statement published on the official website.

Street Institutskaya. The whole world, on this day, sees the horrors that occur on the Maidan -modern technologies allow us, almost broadcast, the real death of people. The confrontation is now taking place in a new channel, open, red year, on the villas paving stones. Here you can see that the street is still wet – the water canal just finished watering ordinary people. The Berkus moved away so that the snipers could work.

This wet paving stone, the only thing that the protesters will see coming back to the camp, to their positions. They just run back down, this one or the other. Feel the cheek of the touch of wet stone, cold as ice, but such a present as nothing else. In this life, at this moment at this second, one can understand that this is already the end. The end is when the ball has already hit. The sound, from the shot, blows the air, no it's not poetry. It's the body that pulls on the ground; it's lifeless; it does not live. What can be felt, to someone who does not know how it is so to see how to pull your child or a brother? When people are getting killed right now. If you do not get up, do not go far, it will be already too late when you understand.

18:00 In the Bureau of forensic medical examination of Kiev 67 corpses were delivered from the morning of February 18th to February 20th, the press service of the Kyiv City State Administration reports concerning the health department. Among them, nine people died in medical institutions subordinate to the Department of Health of the KSCA.

18:16 Bodies of 22 dead protesters are on the territory of St. Michael's Cathedral, where the temporary medical center of Maidan is now located. As the correspondent of Channel 5 reported about 18:00 live, the bodies of the dead were laid on the lawn near the church.

20:12 To prevent the entry of military and titles to Kiev, Maidan activists prepared to block the Obukhovskaya highway. The correspondent of "Espresso reported this.TV". According to the correspondent, now the activists have built a self-made checkpoint from improvised materials: tires, boards, etc. Passenger cars pass through the inspection and, if necessary, block the entire route.

20:25 Poland is ready to receive Ukrainian refugees if necessary. The deputy of the stated this European Parliament from Poland Jan Kozlovsky. "If there are refugees from Ukraine, then we must accept them. This is our duty in the neighboring state "-quotes the words of the parliamentarian."

Interfax-Ukraine "referring to the portal of the Polish" Election Newspaper."

20:50 The EU urged not to introduce a state of emergency and not use the army against the Maidan.

20:55 Among the dead during the clashes between law enforcers and activists in Kiev, 58 people were recognized. Activist Tatyana Pechonchik reported this. Among the dead, there are ten policemen. According to the medical service of the Maidan, as of 18:00 in Kiev, from 70 to 100 people were killed.

21:35 In the Ukrainian Ministry of Internal Affairs they admitted that they used weapons on the Maidan: "To allow the unarmed policeman to get out of the shelling, later armed law enforcers arrived at the scene of the incident. They used weapons as part of the requirements of the Law of Ukraine "On the Police," the ministry's website said.

21:55 EU foreign ministers at an emergency meeting of foreign ministers agreed to impose sanctions against Ukrainian officials "responsible for violence and excessive force." The list of officials may be updated with new names if the situation does not improve.

Ashton also stated that Viktor Yanukovych is responsible for establishing dialogue and stopping violence in Ukraine.

Swedish Foreign Minister Carl Bildt said that the assets freeze and the ban on entry would be "urgently adopted."

22:05 After the meeting with the leaders of the Ukrainian opposition, the Polish, German and French foreign ministers plan to hold another meeting with President Viktor Yanukovych. This was reported on Twitter by the press secretary of the Polish Minister Radoslaw Sikorski.

"After negotiations with the opposition, we must again talk with the president to help the talks.

Progress has been made, but significant differences remain, "the report said.

Recall that the meeting of European ministers and Yanukovych this afternoon lasted almost 6:00, and the president of Ukraine interrupted her for a telephone conversation with Russian President Vladimir Putin.

22:10 In the session hall of the parliament, the "Rada" system was activated, 239 deputies were registered in the room. The meeting is held by Deputy Chairman of the Verkhovna Rada Ruslan Koshulinsky. As a result, the deputies supported the decree in the first reading, which aims to stop the fire and return all security forces to the barracks. For this decision, 233 deputies voted.

This decree obliges to stop the fire, the troops and the Air Force -must return to the places of permanent deployment. The order also prohibits the use of weapons. Also, the resolution prohibits the blocking of transport communications, restricting the movement of transport. The decision notes that only the Verkhovna Rada can introduce a state of emergency.

23:10 Another group of people's deputies left the Party of Regions. Applications for withdrawal from the parliamentary faction.

23:15 Protesters on the Maidan do not diverge. Barricades are considerably strengthened. At the forefront of the fortification on the street. Institutskaya let only people in flak jackets and helmets miss, because, in the opinion of self-defense, they can shoot from the government quarter. The barricades on Maidan have created new stocks of automobile tires, which can set fire in case of an attack by law enforcement.

23:50 Russian President Vladimir Putin considers the representatives of the radical wing of the Ukrainian opposition is guilty of escalating violence in Ukraine. He said this when talking with German Chancellor Angela Merkel and British Prime Minister David Cameron.

00:15 US President Barack Obama accused his Russian counterpart Vladimir Putin of an offensive against democracy in Ukraine. He stated this in Mexico, where the international summit of North American leaders are taking place.

"This is not a competition between Russia and the United States. It's about realizing the hopes and expectations of citizens of Ukraine and Syria to get the main freedoms: freedom of speech, freedom of assembly, transparent and fair elections. The fundamental rights that every Ukrainian and Syrian seeks," said Obama.

21st of February

On the Independence Square in Kyiv, in the morning, a prayer service for Ukraine took place. From the scene, three priests read prayers and baptized people on the square. The atmosphere on Independence is calm.

14:15 The siloviki under the VR are curtailed and settled on buses. Meanwhile, in the BP itself, the break was over, deputies approached the session hall.

16:00 The agreement between the authorities and the opposition on the settlement of the crisis in Ukraine was signed on Friday in Kiev by President of Ukraine Viktor Yanukovich. Leaders of the three opposition factions of the Ukrainian parliament: Vitali Klitschko, Arseniy Yatsenyuk and Oleg Tyagnibok.

The essence of the document was the return to the Constitution of Ukraine from 2004, the constitutional reform, the re-election of the President of Ukraine no later than December of this year. Amnesty to the participants of the clashes, refusal to introduce a state of emergency and conduct of anti-terrorist Operation on the territory of Ukraine, as well as the creation of a coalition government. Prevailing conditions were the absence of the new head of the Interior Ministry, Vitaliy Zakharchenko, and the change of the Attorney General.

The agreement was certified by the European Union President of the Polish Ministry of Foreign Affairs Radoslaw Sikorski and Germany - Frank-Walter Steinmeier, as well as Eric Fournier, Head of the Continental Europe Department of the French Ministry of Foreign Affairs.

16:52, 386 people's deputies voted to return to the Constitution of 2004!

17:10 The Rada passed a law on preventing the persecution and punishment of persons who participated in the events that took place during peaceful assemblies. For voting 372 people's deputies.

17:18 There are tens of thousands of people on the Maidan. People say goodbye to the dead.

The song so penetrates the heart. Creepy shivers run through your body the words convey that it's not just war and not only grief, but it's a battle of good and evil on this earth. The power of any country and the world must understand that this way what does not result in, it's time to Change reality and live according to the laws. It's not too late, and this famous Ukrainian person can change everything now.

Another 28 deputies left the Party of Regions, as well as throughout the country. They write massively about the dismissal and withdrawal from the party of regions of the heads of regional organizations, regional deputies and mayors.

22.40 On Independence Square in Kiev, at these times, the funeral of dead activists is performed. And they say that they "spit on the agreements of the authorities with the opposition" and stand to the full victory and resignation of the government. To which the opposition deputies certainly agree, that they would not have time to recognize there. "To go to the end," that's what the people, the deputies of the opposition deputies and their agreements, have decided.

The next day began with a sense of victory over the regime of the "fifth column" operating on the territory of Ukraine. The people on the streets desired to grab the perpetrators and punish the entire banditsku power, from the Communists and the president.

12:40 Alexander Turchinov was elected Acting President of Ukraine for the period until the elections in May 2014. "For" voted 282 deputies.

Here in the corridors of the tents at night where they're only sit in the cold at the barrel with fire, you can hear the words of truth, futility, and expectation. Standing, by the fire, a watchful speaker said:

"On Maidan, all the people and the screens of TVs could be seen right away, then the slippery and a sweet replay of those who do not precisely change anything, but radically new, does not have because corruption, outrages, and looting have long knotted everything and on human suffering.

Everything seems to be already understandable, and youth and desire and it's time to change, the future to those who already should be enough and enter the history of truth, honor and free land, because all those treasures of this are not worth it".

This morning in the courtyard I met a handsome, high-blooded boy in bandages. I offered help: medicine, clean things, food, to call the doctor. He very politely refused everything and said he was waiting for his students' friends to write a statement to the police. I began to roar. This is someone's baby!! Lord, So he calmed me and then kissed my hands. He brought food to Mikhailovsky.

And now this child saw five channels. He told me. Luba, Madame, everything is fine, we will save UKRAINE! God save our girls and boys

One year later.

Kuzma Scriabin

"Those where they shoot, those where they shoot. Peaceful people are dying. No one cuts it. That is, our policy can be seen as its own on this whole thing. And from me, such a warrior is relative. I'd rather earn in the body and pre-emption those guys who need it. Some people know war affairs better than I do. I've already won my own, but if I get to drink, I'll go where I want to be".

Simply that is ideotoska situation now, terribly ideojaska the case, - I to that explanation simply cannot find.

For what kind of "fuck" sorry, so many people died? I do not understand.

Because none, I wrote letters to the client, he will be on the new album. I did it all.

And the present too.

"Was there a reaction from the president side...?

"They do not consider me at all for any danger." They owe me for such a mole, like any other person in Ukraine so that you can take. You know, vityr and crush.

So, they live on a different planet and every new day comes to that komushki, he falls visually, he stops thinking and thinks. Well, those idiots, they were recognized, they are idiots, and I'm lucky enough to go and row.

Paradox, you understand the mystery in the fact that no one would like to be a hero in that Ukraine.

Well, write down your name in history so that your children will be proud that their grandchildren will say, "God, what a grandfather you were, great-grandfather," Hetman yomayo, do you understand?

Though, do something."

No one, no figures devastation.

Ukrainians are always able to choose one with a vasilino, then, so that even without a vasilin, you know, it's not Teba even running to the pharmacy. We want one to be on zhoshche, you know. Sado mazahism is so in the genes. I also think that not primarily, and the theme works. I believe that the buckwheat scheme works a little, somewhere in the village, and I believe that there is such falsification going on there. That there is a unique way to do it, that we would not even have a choice. To perstavily, yeah, he was on foot, second, third, and now others, but the same.

We were not ashamed of the eye. We were just heads like this, manipoluvals, like strings. I could see those more than two thousand buses standing around Kiev. Well, somebody has to pay for it all, pure, because they came for the fact that they lived there, understandably people helped, but the bulk.

What is not going to the square? For a year, in my opinion, more reasons than Yanukovych, you know.

Killed so many hundreds of heavens, in my every day, the heavenly hundred perish.

We tried to do an acutely social program, a sickle in the eggs and realized that after the second program, we realized that it does not give anything, because we become idle talkers. Just like everyone else. Everyone ascertains the fact, but nothing is done.

I speak with the analyst, I ask him, and what are our chances?

"Well, what chances, it is necessary to control those people who we have chosen.

"Well, how am I going to the deputy... I'll go twice..."

In Ternopil, I tried to get to the deputy. Just the neighboring door from me where I lived was a deputy's deputy; I will not say a bad word. Peter ass relatively.

I look from the first to the third office hours in it. Monday through Wednesday. "It's Monday. I can not do it." In an hour again, "Peter ass is not here, you know? "In another hour, "He still not here."

Well, by a lucky chance, I was there on Tuesday too, from PESHO third time. There is no Peter ass.

He did not become a Peter ass.

I ask that analyst/I had a situation like this, well, he says he should go to the Supreme Council.

I say, imagination. I'm a plumber, with Gradisk. I shrink into the high radar and say, you know. I want to find Petr an ass and ask him a couple of questions. The reaction of the guard of the council of the councils was returned, kicked, you know, only under my ass. Not under the same cat I was looking for and flying back to Gradisk not weakly sobbing, but wasting your time, your money.

I believe that only those young boys who did those investigations yesterday, they can publicize something and may be shaken by someone. There are ideological people, there are many ideological people, just so deep a guilt that those ideological people are so powerless, so this is such a very long process. I think that Poroshenko will also finish that war, that they do not do that.

There is a moment of conscience; you know for sure that Caina also attacked yours, you know for sure that a lot of people are stuck because of that, you know exactly what to be what echi. That you do not understand, well, okay to earn some koportivi, but to ride and those samovars there receive, then the gramophone. I believe that is. Still, I think that this is such a nod towards the empire. I would not do that.

Because you understand, there is no dignity, maybe what kind of weighty I carry, but there is no dignity.

Western Ukraine, refueling, the city of Rovno, shchatschin chanson in Russian, you know, they stand with such bows yellow-blue. That already their feet are plaited, people say, but you are even worse than that Putin is what his car is because he is a car, because you are here and here you are angry from the inside. So this is just a lack of dignity. Mom and Dad did not give, the school was on cymbals, and made its street, that's all. That is an intense process, it hurts me about that, but it's Oman, who knows what about Oman? Oman is a beautiful country. God, as if Ukraine was like one hundredth on it. Drunk at the wheel prison you are of the year; you put the speed on 80 kilometers.

The prison is two years old, the unpacking packing. A prison a week, stole the left point, retook the rights. Criminally zero, even though you are Muslim, also though you are a Muslim, even Orthodox, no one touches anyone, do not go naked. Dubai is such a mess, and Oman is only for people. From Monday to Thursday, then I have a weekend, Iceland is ahead torn, Spitzbogen is just a brain.

America is a people, that's when you're in ambition for more than four days, then you realize that you do not want from there it, they've reached that bastard.

1.1 It was a cold winter evening. Kuzma's interview did not go out of the head. Leaving from Pechersk to Shulyavka all thought what to do next. Money, left on deposit in one of the banks is likely not now return before the deadline. Before the time limit as the bank must give it no longer will. Relocated to another tiny machine-gun, a bit of a ride and decided to go out to walk to the house park. Despite the snow and yellow lanterns, the park seemed dark. A strong man came to meet from afar.

My thoughts were a bruising issue of what to do. I so wanted to return to Ukraine, to live here to go to work, chi my business to run. One has already launched, I contradicted myself. Sending students to study in Canada, and imitation is further. And in this situation in the country, even this business, it does not go.

The man was approaching me and, on his ascent, it was clear that he was going very purposefully.

Although I was also going to freedom quickly and confidence, I was not to occupy myself.

What if I go abroad again. Again, to Canada? No, I do not want to go there anymore. Europe? No, just like traveling there, maybe in the US, Los Angeles? When I was there, I did not like it, and I did not want to go back there ever again. I did not even throw a penny into the ocean. Again, leave his native country with his own home. I have my way, my war, my soul, my heart and mind, Ukraine, and the whole world. From this moment I must live and be what I want to be and must be. I do not want to leave, but only there, I must try to reach the results and say about what is so important to me in the hope that they will hear me.

The man who was going to the meeting was already very close. The path is a little. It seems he is muttering something. We only bumped our shoulders a little.

"Are you alright?" I asked after looking back

"I am sorry," he answered.

The man spoke. His face could not be seen because of the darkness. He apologized to freedom politely, even with some irony in his voice, looking like a well-dressed man. I was almost making a step further. I was in such a strange state as if time stood still around me this whole evening.

"I also. Already I tried to go further, and..."

"I'm sorry very much, again, but will not you have money?"

In my pocket there was a note in 20 UAH, all that I left for life after my arrival from Canada was over.

Of course, there was also a card where parents of the same number used to pay money. This day would be only tomorrow. And why to go to the US, I asked myself in my head.

He turned and walked over to the peasant.

"Here please take two hryvnia, all that is, I hope they will help you than Li Bo. If I could, I would give more, I'm sorry."

"Thank you ... Sorry to have asked you."

"Never mind. Good luck to you; everything will be fine. You'll see."

The man turned and walked on, and I went on too. Such a sadness took me by the heart that a man who is already clearly in his forties goes and so must ask another person what kind of world is this where we are chewing. What kind of country is this? How can this be lived? Do not have to go again.

The night was colder and wintry.

I kept thinking, I was thinking about what to do. All my life the Pope gave me money for everything, again to ask for it? We need to grow up. Well, when there are best friends whom you already know almost half. Even virtually all your life. Lend them, well, when there are real doves, you know for sure that in trouble and joy and you're at them and they can rely on you. Tomorrow I'll go to Kostya, and then to Max. Kostya is one of my best friends from youth. Just this summer, he married Yanochka.

It was already starting to grow light. I went up to the third floor, went into the quartet, turned on the TV turned on the kettle.

Kuzma Scriabin.

I'm stuck in you like a knife

Somewhere between the heart and between two open doors.

According to the official version of the Ministry of Internal Affairs on February 2, 2015, about 8:20 (according to the concert technique of the Skryabin group of Y. Lysyak. It happened around 7:00 according to the investigation, reported by UkrMedia, the call at the substation of emergency medical services was fixed at 6:54 died in a car accident near the village of Lozovatka, Krivoy Rog district of the Dnipropetrovsk region. On the same day, the press service of the Department of the State Automobile Inspectorate of the Ministry of Internal Affairs of Ukraine reported that, according to preliminary data, 86 km of the Krivoy Rog-Kirovograd (48 ° 03'44 " ° 13'25 "east. D.). There was a collision of an SUV Toyota Sequoia, which was driven by a singer and a GAZ-53 milk truck. From the injuries Andrei Kuzmenko died on the spot. Kuzmenko was returning from Krivoy Rog, where on the eve of his group gave a concert. The eyewitness reported that he saw how at high speed in the place of rounding the road jeep musician drove to the oncoming lane and crashed into the side of the tank. An eyewitness suggested that the black Honda was chasing a white jeep. It is assumed that the singer's car was traveling at a speed of 160 km / h. Although local drivers say that it is dangerous to overclock 60 Km/ h on this stretch of the road. The eyewitness noted that there was ice on the track and cars were trying to leave. In the fatal accident, two women have also injured: passengers of the Kuzmenko car and the milk truck, respectively; they were taken to Krivoy Rog hospitals No. 2 and No. 9. The driver of the milk truck during the whole time of the investigative actions was on the scene of the accident.

There are many versions on the Internet; it was not an accident, but a contract killing. The witness of the crash confirms this version. At the same time, Andrei's parents asked not to speculate on the death of a son.

Now all this is remembered, somehow differently. The emptiness that has appeared in the soul, heart, mind has been recognized forever. This is how to lose a native person chi arc. Only you do not cry, do not take up butila, because you understand, this is a void that will always be with you. Now it does not pour, then we all are not eternal. This cousin had her way and lived and did everything for the sake of something more for people, all those songs that are, only the best and to be precise.

Ten days later I said goodbye to my relatives and left for a taxi to the airport. My father watched me on the trail. I said goodbye to him last when he was examined at the hospital. My heart was in the language of my native country, from the fact that I'm leaving. At the front, I still have time to go, but I'll try as I would on the Maidan with the word.

Four years later.

It's been four years; it is 2017. Can anyone understand how this is? Chitiri long years of war, each time people kneel, not only on the square but throughout Ukraine, wherever it is the village of Chi-Town. People fall, chi full pains drop, and everyone on their knees, seeing off the path of heroes enraged our time. People chant in a low voice, "Geo does not die, Heroes do not perish, but also a song, now it has become the voice of sadness. The way heroes see off; it's not just like Chopin's music that uselessly throws us into a cold fear, that we are all dying. These people with an understanding of the beard in life leave us to heaven ahead of time".

Carry the coffin between the people.

Duckling floats on Tisyna

The song of death, everything else is not essential. Mothers cry violently. People ask God to pardon a person, sacrificed themselves, for the sake of others. The benefit that we do not appreciate so much and cannot get to the full. In such cabins soaked with pain and suffering. If God exists, chi some power of the universe, why is it so important to us? Why such a bloodthirst? Because if it does not exist, then we have twice as much work as before. And you are all with your thoughts with your fears, and in the primary existence, as observers of what is happening. I am on the screens of our life. It can happen like this. Please, have mercy on you. Look at the men, on their knees, look at the track of that grave with the hero, it seems to you far away. Neither this happens now, even if you are far beyond the ocean. Human Indifference now kills no fewer weapons in the war. We all now already must fight for our minds knowing what's going on. To be yourself in full and for yourself, to be selfish is not evil, everyone should be in favorable conditions, straightforward things understanding. Rejection of fear and evil are imposing in our daily lives. New nanotechnologies can give us real freedom and power for all on earth. We can all be at the mercy of those who control us now and so far, not so carefully. Sooner or later, our indifference and the propaganda of the head filled with propaganda from all sides will not leave us the choice to fall into a new trap, to the old familiar embrace of death.

In our mother Ukraine, and at all times we stood up and fought and with the gentlemen and the King only afterward with the Communists and fascists, with the Vsesma. That's why enemies all around, from the very beginning, everyone fought in the war, with a spear and a bare ass, years, and we are all in the war, and even Jesus did not stop this chi, Muhammad. All who believe, at least a little, really I need to understand that this is one faith so that I will be both a Christian and a Muslim, not a single person in the world which slogans in our time should not go and in byvati. We all already have a long time to start fighting only with words and only in the right direction.

Because what is happening now, no words or tears of human is not enough. When the authorities are profitable, it seems that the patriots of our future suddenly did not turn around. Washed away those who sit in the rear, so maybe we had the Ilovaisky cauldron. When the enemy is set against its people, and the Slavs, who have all been fought against the truth on the side of those who exploit them.

When people living in the material world do not own their lives. When everyone is killing himself and his brain, alcohol drugs light and not very, as well as honoring the legal thawed dope and does not see anything even this. When we are all hostages of painted pieces of paper and medals, the numbers on the screen, we are all in the mud of the modern world invented to own us. We all have long deserved the future, so let's save ourselves, all around us and reach the high peaks that we now find even tricky or even impossible to imagine. What can be done with us, if we follow the right path, after ten years, and already 100 years, it is difficult even to imagine. All this is a great revolution that can tick us, if we all unite, also if in the existing Cain, as the decentralization of power, let everyone reconciles. Let everyone get peace and everything that could be wished, maybe even hope if he and God will meet and see him with his living eyes.

Kiev, green chestnuts, just passed a light rain, the sun has already begun to warm the asphalt in the podezd. The smell of summer air so inspires, and it seems that how beautiful this life is. You sit in the usual car and the sound of the motor, the conventional engine pleases, you turn on the radio.

Here's the intersection, you must turn. So, the usual Kiev intersection of roads, Ivan Franko and Bogdan Khmelnitsky, which seems to me even very symbolic, becomes very special for someone who has just seen everything the same as we. Who are all the same as us, but only NOT then when it is blown up, for what he did. Pavel Sheremet, the leading reporter of the publication, "Ukrainian Truth." A man who fought for the truth, in all its senses, and therefore was a completely exceptional person in our time.

"The problem with Ukraine lies in the fact that these oligarchs have completely monopolized certain spheres of the economy. Until then, in Ukraine, it will not be possible to defeat these oligarchs, small and large in different spheres of the economy. Not what economic growth will not be. Oligarchs preserve poverty. " said Pavel Sheremet.

As for Putin's regime, Sheremet did not choose words either. He was friends with Nimtsovim, investigated the murder of the Russian Oppositionists.

This speech, the listeners heard a few months ago. Sheremet's program was closed, and he said goodbye to the empire.

-"I sometimes regret that I'm not Ukrainian. Now God gave us fate gave, such a chance, a significant opportunity for Ukraine. I urge you to be active in public life, to be active at all. To put things in order around yourself and bring order to the country. All the best to you - we will break through!!!"

TSN news In Ukraine and Pavel Sheremet says goodbye to Independence Square. Kiev people all day brings flowers at the place of murder. Paul Sheemet will be buried in his native Minsk.

"There is nothing better than fighting for justice."

"Do you know what this justice is?"

"Either to live by honor or not to live at all and what is it by honor and justly you always know yourself, not prefer to notice, because it's easier to live. So, my friend, it's easier. It's not as it should be, although it's easy to live for someone who lives by honor and craves justice. By the fact that such a person knows why he lives and the moment of life is not a burden. Tygost that cannot understand but carries with him a man with the life of the existing, and not obrešego. An awareness of this comes to everyone, to some of them, too late. At this moment, someone dies, kogotov, and do kill. What are you doing? For the sake of what we live, if not for the sake of what to fix everything? At least correct yourself. Bread and spectacle: World Cup 2017 showed two sides of the medal that the country whose power is heartlessly stealing and makes to lead the Nishibrod existence of its people and carries only death by its authority since the history of Chechnya and our time and who knew from grandfathers with whom? With Ukraine. Yes, we gave birth to your land, so that you steal our history, we became brothers in the Second World War, having been bored with the evil of fascism, and you must with your rotten komunizm harbun in your back. But nothing we will drag your brothers from the horror of their horror which has horror among modern power systems. Despite all the hatred for you, I ask Ukrainians to forgive those who do not understand who are now against us; they are captives of their mistakes and mistakes. I forgive yourself for the fact that the West can not either wake up from what is hiding and become its essence to the end of those who should be like we are in Ukraine."

"If Rosia, as a wicked boy who was trying to prove something, is not justified in not understanding what he is doing. The West understands what is happening, he is no longer a teenager, but so far he is not a man in the head with a drug and alcohol. He can and strike yes understands that to beat the children of the foolish people like Rosia now does not help and tries to riddle them and teach them, but does not show by their example of how it should be."

"We are in the pit of the crook of the grave guys in the bud of the last chance in Ukraine; we are trying to get out of there where the corpse of Syria is already lying. A huge corpse of Africa is rotting nearby, where the authorities only in violence and infection from AIDS."

"The plague of our houses was a war in the world of religions. New troops are preparing stronger than the Egil. If we do not make money all the time, we will not build a new efficient system. We are all killed in a deep rotting common grave by ourselves in Hell, laying our way already in the world that may not exist."

Maybe, therefore, the Russians do not understand us Ukrainians and our hymn they do not have enough understanding to determine how Ukraine has not yet died, fame or freedom.

We all must gather and overcome ourselves and all the evil in the land-our house and perk up in the spirit and become those who must be built an effective system of life. As one single mechanism, and these creatures will answer for cola in the war, for Amsterdam, for that that Crimea Ukrainian prosrali.

Putin is crap, so all football stadiums of the country are shouting at the screamers, they are singing a song. You would see, when the second side of the medal that football and garbage competitions and the world, not depending on what should prevail over us is the only system that carries although at least some hope for the future, there can be so many fans in the world for this.

Such a system of a productive future was in the USSR. This is what my grandfather after the war tried to build a healthy and honest life. For example, he worked after the war in the factory and built roads.

We all must now build a new world and work hard every day. Such work is valid only when there is no phantom of communism of rotten flesh, like power in Russia, Africa, Egil. If you are not, Mr. Putin then proves that anyone in Russia could be in your revenge. You are no more deceitful if you can marry their faces. The more you and no one else can achieve, the one thing is to change everything and build the system altogether. You will be turned 360 degrees from your course, or there is no the sense in your existence, but you could go really with those who are now also at power in the world be reduced to sufficient round-the-clock work for the benefit of every person on this earth.

Where we are all together, the first will determine the path and build eternal system communism. The present without a wrist, in the whole world, to which all countries of the world will agree since the idea of equality and prosperity for all is a ghost of the path by which the material world. Although communism would have been faster, if not rozvaltsya, and why, because it's funny. There was not enough compliance. So all, do not go by patience and suffering for the sake of victory. We do not shy go by the strength of the material world and the effectiveness of management. This is the business that will graft us to what the communism in the USSR was pushed to.

No more need to run and fight like a boy, what would have been considered in the world where you are seen for such a thing. For not foresight or are already going to war, and we will not cast you out of the wild as the generation of Russi and Herod, and kill, giving life to 150 million. Who, back in the old world, deserved to live appropriately and safely.

People all over the world, the earth is very little, if everything goes on like this. There is no choice ; all the authorities that cannot be depleted need to be dethroned to join the effective general system ; this applies to everyone. We all know that even Germans can explode with anger like a people, is the only question for what? For the sake of dining all of us, Russia, Ukraine, the US, Germany, all, and then you only in words, and Ukraine was the first to give up its nuclear weapons. You were our guarantors, only the Budapest format is permissible !!! as well as the return of the Crimea? Yes, but forget you about the borders, there are no more borders on the earth, we are all one. Now everyone decides for themselves, dine themselves and do everything yourself those who understand otherwise cannot be, only for the sake of world peace and procreation on earth. I do not know that we shouldbecome one, a modern plant, like Ilona Mask, only one person and faith in him will not help, we need an effective system that does not change the replacement of pyrimene sums.

If we do not change the criteria for assessing human performance, if, thanks to the requirements that liberal philosophy offers for us.

The end is in hell because if in the human mind, the distances between truth and lies are reduced.

If, as the idea of postmodernism suggests, there is no truth, and there is a pluralism of opinions, then the most terrible thing happens: the border between good and evil is erased. After all, in the context of the pluralism of the views that allow the consideration of truth and lies on one level, allowing for the idea of moral relativism, everything is possible. Then the question of political technology, mass media, creation of a standard under the general educational process. If the task is set, these false and dangerous messages. Today, we consider drugs, alcohol, and so on evil, but the main question is: what will the next generations view as evil. Whether they will not forget all the Ten Commandments, and what can they come to?

Because the commandment "not to kill" under different pretexts is already violated many countries?

We, the people, will be able to reach a compromise, determination in the choice of life and rights, and jointly provide a future that we can be proud of.

And no matter how long and responsible the way for us is, I understand and accept with my mind that in all these disputes: in the upbringing of the child, in the economy, in politics, in world politics and in seeing the goal for which we live. Even in the dispute over disputes, as well as in the decision within oneself. Who to be or not to be in this life, and whether to live or not to live, the main thing is to realize that we are all here on the planet Earth. We, the kind that lives life, which dissolves in blood and love, in alcohol and kindness, in drugs and death, in crime and joy, in sex and lies.

I do not tell you, "Believe in God," but if you do not believe, then see for yourself how you live. If you do not understand simple logic, then what can you talk about with the people who stand before me?

I want to remind you that we are all people, we are all people. Each of us is a person and an individual, and if all of us, or most of us, want to live like people, just a kind of where we can not do without.

We should be able to talk, discuss, make collective decisions that will carry the right choice, even in the most basic framework for world society. But at the same time, all find a compromise that would stop all that must be protected in a peaceful existence that will not affect a healthy, young generation, which itself will determine for itself. How to live with them, looking at the example of their ancestors, not just to be born and live a little, to beat the dead. How it can happen in the modern world, and each

of those who did not touch it, of course. When he sees or hears about such, thanks to the fate that he cannot live in fear, but this fear of the thought will pass away in a second, and the person will say: "Well, it means that it's not lucky that I can do it?" And I'll say: if you're not someone, then you can do nothing.

And if the world community decides on bans, which are genuinely for good and justified, then it must be banned or stopped. I do what I could, and every day I do it every day, trying to embody the truth, in reality, my dreams, and ideas. I want to live; I want to love with my whole heart again and enjoy it, despite all the lessons and tests that bring us destiny, life, God. That we take only the best and draw conclusions, designed for each of us personally.

In each of the seconds that await us, but imagine only. Every second that has just passed and now exists. About one hundred people die like us, so I want to create and be the creator of myself. The one that should be, who will cherish each second and be worthy of every moment of existence. Even if my heart is stopped now, then consider that my star has caught fire in a new life in which there is already. What you are doing this second and what it is for you, what are you bringing to this world?

Our life is like a star in the night sky: one is shining so, and the other is different. Their radiance the time is instant and at the same time an eternity. It's impossible to take them: thoughtless, empty, maybe bright, blind - flying into darkness, godlessly, interrupted only by themselves. Looking at it, you'll shout in a whisper, guessing at the desires possible. No, I do not want to be like that! In a word, the time had an eternity, but eternity does not have time.

The eternal dawn will be closed by a white wing, as if there were none and, notice, with a new sunset,will not.

And for everyone whose star is lit, the sky will open a new night, giving them time eternity, so decide what you want to be: a bright moment, flying in darkness, or a star glowing forever, or maybe the master of the universe. Those who bridled it all, alive, those who survived and those who have found the whole the essence of truth and purity, thereby deserving of prevailing over everything. Being one with everything, because we are now in the step to this and at the same time in the second from death and in such astate of affairs by the standards of the existence of the universe we have seconds, only 50-100 Earth years.

For this, all that was meant fought all our generations of those who are now calling themselves a Ukrainian and continue to fight. Now in the war our knights-the Cossacks, we should be such Cossacks in everything. In every issue, in every thought in the struggle for oneself and just this, the immensely struggle on the side of ethical, justice, and honor, I will not be otherwise. We must all become real children who are worthy of their father creator.

The wind blows it's twisting in the field, in the area of the Chumata, among the stars, which the Cossacks watch on the road.

Words, words are just ordinary sounds or the only thing that you can give forever to another person, knowing that they were not empty, and in them, you are all. But there is no answer, the emptiness in it has acquired peace, insensitivity or just misunderstanding.

But how can it be, no, I will not believe it ever, because this candle should burn in it just like in all of us, maybe even a little bit, still smoke?

People like ships

Cause to become the heroes of that war

They wanted very much

Refrain:

Proudly swimming and nobody believes

That evil is interested in him

And among the winds, we don't hear the rats

That is gnawing through our bottom

....

poet and musician Kuzma Skryabin.

Now it's 2018. Ukraine since the beginning of Crimean anecdies and wars with the Russian occupying and members of the armed forces in the east still destabilize the sitka, Putin does not want to exchange everyone for everyone. Our Crimean Oleg Sintsov at this moment is starving the 99th day in Siberia, unlawfully arrested. Like hundreds of other citizens of Ukraine. His only condition of hunger for Putin is to release all Ukrainians and those who have been illegally issued. Not by their own will issued a Russian passport. People in the Crimea continue to disappear and are under constant threat of arrest and any other arbitrariness of the non-autocratic power that takes any measures to the Tatar people and Ukrainians who represent the majority of the population of the peninsula. They consider themselves to be Ukrainians or belonging to the Ukrainian state, yet at the same time. They perfectly speak the Ukrainian language, of course, as well as Russian. Mezhlis the only stronghold of confrontation, which is continuously under arbitrariness and pressure. Often people take away the real estate business, do not agree with anything, or disappear or are given a gesture and torture. It was as though the Stalinist times of repression had returned. The peninsula is under sanctions, and finally, one can not even pay an online account by any international payment system.

When the war broke out, we all got bored, the leading indicator of this was the voluntaristic dipping. This is so important as what the Ukrainians did who became volunteers and stopped the enemy, defended their homeland, defended their lives. For 4 and a half years every day, they were not killed in the war less than three of our soldiers, our brothers, our eternal heroes. The terrible reality in which we live and to which the millions of people in the world do not pay attention. The power is insane in Ukraine. At first, it was because of them that we had such phenomena as the Ilovaisky cauldron, where thousands of our volunteers were surrounded. The power, which it is advantageous to bury there the best sons of Ukraine and with the help of war, tries to retain control and plunder the country. The people and, most importantly, do not have an active policy and economic conflict. They destroy our dream in Ukraine, but they will not succeed, and we will change this forever. These bastards of the Soviet Union, as well as throughout the post of the USSR, were given to people when they sank. Then where they were in power and massively began to privatize and to steal the common national property, which was a strategic chain in filling the general supply. The people that had and were part of everything in their majority became not even anyone, but a corrupt part of the life of the state when everything had to be asked for money from those who managed to pre-privatize state property and then to steal. People thus became slaves of the country in which the businessmen and rulers of laws and business were singled out to the politic stratum, which undoubtedly resides in tini in Ukraine. The people indeed must even after the year now receive compensation from all that was common, including sharing profits, which was earned by those who were such pre-privatizers and are 80% of Ukraine's list of forces.

Of course, as at the beginning of the formation were those real patriots who did everything that Ukraine would gain independence. They wanted to build a stable Ukraine. So, they killed Chernovil, Gongadze, Kuzma.

Our salvation, as a country, as a people in the only chance to build a new economic system. Those who killed and survived in the division can be so easily disregarded, what belongs to the people, even though they are sick, some of them and they could become the founding fathers. By the example of the USA of a strict business state and give real freedom to people that in the modern world measured by welfare and material provisions. State servants of the people should do so that the violence of Ukraine will become free. Make the state servants of the people whose people should be selected by the people among the same people like themselves. Not among the businessmen of the same suit in the law.

Even when we win in the struggle for Ukraine, the whole world still does not move in the system of joint coordinates. We all need to be reduced to the current price world of the standard method of active management, mutual relations, providing the absolute of an extended network of work of efficiency.

Efficiency is our goal in everything.

The wind blow. it's twisting in the field, in the area of the Chumata, among the stars, which the Cossacks watch on the road.

Words, words are just ordinary sounds or the only thing that you can give forever to another person, knowing that they were not empty. In them, you are all. But there is no answer, the emptiness in it has acquired peace, insensitivity or just misunderstanding, and therefore death.

But how is it, no, I do not believe in this ever, even though this candle does not burn, but the embers cherish. This means that Ukrainians and all people stand and warm their hands, but that's for now while they all contain let us take the fire of revolutions for real life, peace, love. All the people on the ground, or anything from all that nothing remains, not even a word.

The ruby sparks of the dusk sun: the memory of maydan !!!!!!! The time when we all start to feel that we can change this world !!!!!!!

Planes became a new threat of the spread of viruses and diseases, with global warming, more and more conditions will develop, and it is one more threat for humanity. Do you know who went for this war in Ukraine? Heroes, namely ordinary teachers and managers. And also, regular guys, as I which, just grew or grew, and even farmers and all most ordinary people, fathers, brothers, sisters (female battalion). Of course, these people are not ordinary. It is the people, the best in the world, who at the right time takes a step forward. Such feeling that all as if do not see that horror that occurs in the world.

To you not understand all this pain, horror. That the most ridiculous that turns out to the majority to the population all the same on what occurs. To you, all the same until it concerns, someone from you. It will affect all of you, can even, almost altogether, in at one time and then all of us will regret that we were so indifferent, so are not smart, so careless. As all of you got me.

I want to ask you forgive Ukrainians all to them – who killed you with that and forgive me that I ask you about it. I ask you and Tatars, Poles, Russians, Germans, residents of Afghanistan, Turkey, Romania, China to forgive. Also, I invite you to forgive everyone with whom you were at war. Let the whole world, all who were at war will forgive each other. And in memory of what was cherish this peace, I hope, you do not learn, what is it, that right now someone from your family is killed or hold captive, do not learn as it.

I didn't tell details of the heroic battle of millions of people in World War II, but I heard a couple such from the grandfather, honestly, a lump in a throat. Unless all of us didn't deserve that we had what all of us dream of unless we deserved to have what we have now? It is a rhetorical question because it is Hell just some, but not the mother Earth. To your socialism and let it is terrible and has to be, of course, yours faithfully who already lives in these the countries, but people have to live in each corner of the world equally well. Then nobody anywhere at all would go. All of us have to solve these problems at once one front. The Triliad companies and all rich men of the world also have to unite and to become an integral part of the process of the solution of world problems. Now we play rat games in a ship hold. Beginning from the poisoning with Skripali with the Russian law enforcement agencies. A shame of political system in the world and the gangster and terrorist movement, which including the own people occupied, even before the occupation of the Crimean Peninsula in Ukraine. The only thing that saves and shows that everything is possible to us everything will unite - sanctions of the USA and front a part in the West. The only rescue of people and all countries of association in the uniform force and mutually control absolutely in everything and at everyone. When the power of system eats such terrorists, both in the biggest mash-tabs, and to a small, but very painful abscess on an organism of a small business or just in the lane of any of the street on the planet.

I am an ordinary person as each of the people in this world. I try to make myself. Of course, I, as well as everything, am not rather useful in considering myself at least by that who can control wholly himself in life, political views, religion. All of us know that the past so breaks a set of us, and this new history at everyone the, as well as the truth, but all of us are heroes of our time, without any implication now. If today to ask me that I think. Will I answer? Request my favorite movies? I will answer it. I have many favorite movies, but the time we speak about history, its necessary to notice that there are two outstanding *One of the Men* and the American version go into the battle *We Were Soldiers*.

In the first movie, as well as in the second is shown what friendly people fought for ideas of this world. Our both societies, not about these movies, united and thoroughly mixed up in the states. The most different sectors of society united for the sake of one common good goal. It is necessary to notice that in the USSR, incredibly different, but at the same time such similar people to one country. As well as in America, by the way nevertheless in the fight for independence against Germany still united.

Sixty years its undoubted development peak in the USSR. By the way, at the beginning of the 60th, Valery Vasilyevich Lobanovsky won the Championship of the USSR, the Champions League about Dynamo Kyiv and USSR national team.

The USSR united all countries in one and people so mixed up that is not important any more what truth of history was before and can because of it in Ukraine people survived. After Famine-Genocide as many had apartments in Moscow and to the relatives in parcels sent crackers that they didn't die of hunger. Others were lucky to survive, after all having hidden, though something from the Red Army.

In Ukraine as well as in Kazakhstan where how I know, remains an unconfirmed fact. 1931-1933, more than once its mentioned cannibalism these years. After everything that was in the 60th, the country is full-fledged, but Cold War of the USA and the USSR began. Now in modern Russia, it's possible to claim that this war continued with a new force. In then in the territory of Vietnam and Afghanistan, then currently in the area of Syria and Ukraine.

All of us are brothers in this world, and all of us will unite in a modern history what those who would be, to look, read about it, knew that we made something that just in a leg to ours today. The speech delivered from the movie will be the ideal word: "We were soldiers" It would be desirable to write all till that time, the war in Vietnam didn't begin yet. Further, I made light understanding that almost same horror occurs at me in the homeland now.

How here not to remember that who died that American senator and to what he did is this life as it lives.

John Sidney McCain the third was hit in Vietnam by the Soviet military for what has been awarded a red star which has also died from cancer. McCain spent five years in captivity, but then a year later returned and became the most famous American in Vietnam and in every possible way helped this and to other countries which were at war for a right cause. Where violated human rights, cane to the Maidan during the revolution.

Now a weather forecast on TV. I'm confident in one; we can save ourselves, can for this planet already late, but people perhaps. We will not leave anybody when there are Mars and then Moon when as on giving all will gather in the countries and from there, in turn, are among themselves evacuated.

Everything can be if we don't save our earth. For this purpose, its necessary to all of us will unite in a single whole, in the system, almost similar to soccer. There is one person who became an example of such an order. Though the system, on that and network, but isn't one person, especially weapon not to change anything anymore. Today as all were at war when it's honest also for them, only those who, we have to analyze at most each law today and fight for each word as in soccer fight for each ball. The system of total soccer has to be the system of whole life where each participant an integral part of the mechanism under the name of human society. Then the problem of each person will be solved, from And to I. Where everything will be honest.

Where each of us will understand separately that it's correct and to act as the right to vote that so or so (still Shakespeare spoke about similar). The soccer is the peak of art for men; it is the third symphony by Beethoven, it is theatre and the super movie with the scenario which is difficult for guessing. Only knowing everything and having created an ideal system with mutually control such that there in the ear an interrelation ball. Our planet is even similar to a ball; we kick it to and for one of the stories as Roman will not end yet. Today different time, we are capable, with new technologies to consider and hear everyone without any falsification even of children of 5 years that too have the right to vote and the correct calculation from percent of the proposed solution of this or that country. All of us on a threshold of defeat and a victory, as in the final. All of us have to become ideals of a sports way of life.

I have left to this world the world of soccer saw what disorder occurs here, can just because of this game. Already so many countries endured associations without borders, it shows a way, though at the same time we understand that all have to understand its details. Soccer, of course, no such level, but the real trainer knows problems and possibilities of everyone and helps to find a way to self-realization and ideal completing teams. The words of Lobanovsky, the most titled trainer, the most titled club of the USSR Dynamo Kiev. Even the average team with tactics of total soccer will beat a group of stars.

Only contain everything in the world we force."

It's what was the national idea of the USSR contains to one purpose, the better future, but somewhere on the way, we lost it. Corruption won against the system under the name Communism and Americans there is nothing here, everyone in the place appeared in a situation from the crime of tops to survive and save the family. Itself made decisions to become the bride taker or the corrupt official. Whendemocracy doesn't cope with drugs in life of the society, here indeed a trace of KGB, but in the same way, everyone on places made decisions. It became clear that Democracy as the system became obsolete.

Now Russia on the way to communism, but they at the same level as Imperial Russia and overthrows of the tsar Nicolai 2. America to acceptances, still declarations of independence about the remoteness of the continent where the countries more than the States in the USA kept and removed the system of a material world. At this stage Democracy became obsolete, but understanding that this system indeed impaired all of us, of course with the same example as the system of the USSR to the association in socialism is the future of our world which can save us only worldwide. Where diplomats battle and if though someone somewhere told lies in the country to the people. Also in the other country who told lies to other people, its called a mistake in the system only the global platform where speak all the truth all languages. We must recognize errors, and errors are corrected all of us will be able to understand this world, to resolve any issue, to eradicate the evil of a precept Bozhey. Oh, do not tell lies.

Only present what ideal society we can become what all of us contain can reach. To me, never to forget those dreams of the childhood that I play soccer. Soccer is not a game and not a religion. It's the whole the life which because of trauma can stop or because of age and shows that everything is temporary, longer than all the rest and always only the system wins. Our life so is in a shadow of these bright lives of cinema and sports that behind this light that is not visible who is in a shadow. There the whole world which should be lit with the view of honestly. Of a factor competitive at us is enough factor, us all should define the purpose. For example, the general association and rescue, and further everyone now and making any new decisions realize whether correctly you do and begin every one with yourself. You know to change the world, to help him to become better. We have to change first of all ourselves to become the best version of! Without rage, not to contents, grief. All these emotions are shown in our life repeatedly, and the more we feel them. The worse we do for ourselves and the world! How many bitterness, has got down, aggression in this word! Why do people want to be at war? For what?

It doesn't preserve the peace at all! So we only kill him! We kill ourselves. We kill the world! We must change everything we must to fix our word! We need to make a new system. We must to make realignment, one currency, and inclusive development and benefit around the world. This is what all our generations in Ukraine spar for and the whole history of humanity in the struggle for it in essence.